Out From My BooX

Rajnish G Shirsat

First Published by

ISBN: 978-93-5611-509-5

BLUEROSE PUBLISHERS
www.bluerosepublishers.com
info@bluerosepublishers.com
+91 8882 898 898

About the Author

But I'm not an author. I didn't write this book with a script in mind, any character built around. All this was straight from my heart. My mind drove the thoughts, and the pen wrote it.

I did my schooling at Christ Church School, Mumbai, the only one amongst the two ICSE Board schools Mumbai had. That was a strong vision of my parents to put me in. I grew up in a very humble surrounding in south Bombay (Mumbai was then called Bombay) and soon moved to the suburbs of Santacruz. It was here I indeed met a variety of people from different religions and backgrounds. I graduated in Commerce stream and completed my Diploma in Business Management, short courses from IIM, Bangalore, and FIEO (Federation of Indian Exports Organization). I started my professional career in 1992 in Repro India Limited, where I spent a significant part of my career. Here, I learnt a lot of things, met my mentor Dushyant Mehta, and picked up little gems from Romi Vohra and Mukesh Dhruve.

Eventually, I started my print management and consulting business under the banner of R&S Enterprises with my business partner, Swapnali Haryan, who has been with me all along, contributing with her exceptional organizational skills.

Contact me at:
Email: rajnish9shirsat@gmail.com
www.facebook.com/RajnishGS
www.linkedin.com/in/rajnishshirsat

Preface

How do you measure success? How do you know you have reached a level you think has given you career satisfaction of any sort?

When we start our careers, few understand and know when it has begun. For many, it begins when they participate in their family business just by getting exposed to the environment. The parents, uncles, brothers all discuss business matters over the dinner table, and for them, their business journey starts there.

Many would remember some significant event that gets stamped on the mind forever. It could be the clinching of that massive deal with the followed celebrations or a consequential loss that disrupted the family's fortunes forever. For a working professional, it could be the MBA degree he acquired from a premier business school or for that familiar person of average educational background who starts his career not by plan but by chance.

The journey of my professional career started unplanned and by chance. I simply happened to be at that right place at the right time.

I've read a few autobiographies and read great books by authors like Subroto Bagchi, Jim Collins, Robin Sharma, Peter Theil, and many more who inspire me. Their books always taught me something. This book of mine is an effort to give the reader something that can provide him with courage, teach him to be street-smart, and develop an attitude to adapt and get inspired from day-to-day events that lead us to something or the other. As they say, a book's strength is not about the content entirely, but it's about what the reader can take away from it.

Please do write to me if this book connects with you.

I thank my father, who has been my biggest inspiration, my mother for guiding me constantly, my wife for her unconditional love and support, my daughter, brothers, and my sisters for being always encouraging and Milind Maloor, my dear friend who has helped me in shaping up this book.

Rajnish G Shirsat

February 2022

Introduction

Some events shake you up. If I have to even mention something like the dates of 9/11 or the year 1947 or the reforms of India, a picture does emerge in our mind.

One such event was the Budget speech of India's Finance Minister. In 1991, India's Shri Manmohan Singh abolished the Licence Raj, a source of slow economic growth and corruption in the Indian economy for decades. He liberalised the Indian economy, allowing it to speed up development dramatically.

Little did I realize then, when I was in my last year of graduation in 1992, how these reforms made by our finance minister would affect many young who started their careers and me. Post these reforms, how we would now have to deal with competition, develop the art of selling to a hungrier and choosier customer. I proudly say I'm a product of the new liberalized economic India. I started my career in this era.

Till 1991, we had a Bajaj scooter for which we had to wait for several years to get delivery after booking; the same was the case with a landline telephone which was an item of an elite class, the brands were limited, the choice was minimal, the packaging and designing on the brands didn't matter as they do now.

We saw everything changing overnight after this historic Budget. Foreign Institutional Investors started pouring in money. The stock markets liberalized further to allow companies to raise money through public issues. The banks got privatized, and many such developments made the communication, print, media, and advertising industry noticed.

Corporates started caring for brand building, retail shelves were gaining importance, creativity became a serious business, and in all this, the print industry gained tremendous momentum. With this came the need for salespeople in the print industry. As they say, insurance is never sold, but it's always bought, but in the case of the print industry, it needed people to sell print more seriously. It became an art.

Did I plan my entry in Sales? No. What was I getting into, and what made me enter Sales? I was lucky I landed at the right place. Did I plan to be in the print industry? No.

After quitting to be a Chartered Accountant in the first fifteen days of my Articleship, I, fortunately, realized that's not my cup of tea. I couldn't see myself sitting for hours in one chair. I'm an extrovert, a person who wants to meet people, go out in the markets, visit, feel the pulse of what's happening on the ground, and what better than Sales as a profession?

It was in December 1992 I got selected for a Walk-in-interview. I honestly didn't know which company it was for; all I knew was, it was for sales trainees, and it was an opening I was looking for. I didn't think it was for a printing company. The brief introduction given to us in an open forum was very confusing. I could see a chart put up on the wall with a few arrows pointing towards the products and services it was offering. With this understanding, I entered the markets to sell. It was evident I wanted to be in Marketing & Sales.

My first encounter with "selling" was when I assisted my sister, running a ready-made clothing business participating in local exhibitions. I was her brand builder, promotional help, stock-keeper, and designer in setting up her stalls in the shows to sometimes help in selling, often interacting with ladies of all kinds.

In this new liberalized India, I was meeting customers of all kinds. They were demanding, hungry for more options, and price-sensitive. Everything around them in their business was vibrant, dynamic, and promising for growth. They expected vendors to also be of their wavelength. They wanted salespeople who could understand their requirements, think on their feet and robustly service them.

The markets shaped me up; the new India made me learn on the job, taught me what works and what doesn't and most importantly, how to sow seeds for future growth based on relationships.

These sixteen quotes are self-made that I realized have stayed with me forever, and then it hit me one day to shape them into a book. I have been learning, failing, trying again, working hard, and finally tasting success all along this journey.

I hope this book inspires people especially who are establishing themselves in sales as a career. In business, for me all are in Sales – you have to earn money for the business, everything else is a cost.

Happy reading.

Contents

1. Consult - never Sell

It was in December, the winter of Mumbai if we can call that by any extent. Till then, I used to wake up for my college and then head for it around eleven in the morning. I was a fun-loving person with many college friends, and life was running smoothly.

I woke up to the alarm set for six in the morning, looked into the mirror while brushing my teeth, and saw a confident man staring at me. I was getting ready for a new phase in my life, a new chapter to be opened. I smiled back at the man in the mirror, gathered myself, and said, you can do it. I had already undergone a massive transformation in my life just three years ago when my father expired. I matured dramatically after his death and became more responsible, looking after my mother, grandmother, brother, and sister though I was the youngest amongst all. This quality of taking responsibility early in life helped me throughout my career.

My mother knocked on the bathroom door to say the breakfast was ready, and I hurriedly finished off my bath and was out. New trousers and a neatly pressed shirt waited for me in my cupboard. It was a gift from my mother for my first day at work.

I reached office well before time, a quality which has stayed with me till date. No matter what the situation, no matter what the mode of commuting, the Mumbai chaos, traffic, etc. I can proudly say I was never late for any of my appointments, meetings whether official or casual with clients or with clients, in all my twenty-five years of professional life. I prefer going there before time, say at least ten to fifteen minutes, settling down, using the washroom, organizing myself perfectly before being called for the meeting or appointment. This trait of managing my time well has helped several times. It gives you more time for yourself; you don't have to rush and get rattled up. It also gives you time to settle on the table. You know where the papers are, the calculator, the scale, the note-pad, visiting card, and you are waiting for the other person who finds you with a smile on your face. Imagine what can happen if you are late.

The dark corridors of any industrial estate can demoralize the best of energetic people. I was no exception, and imagine it was my first day. Our office was located in the prime central area of Lower Parel in Mumbai. It was in an industrial estate that was considered the hub of the printing industry. In a way, it was a vast factory comprising of small units of entrepreneurs, each having a set of machines required to complete the print job. Owners of these units knew eachother well and would happily support eachother to fulfil customers' requirements.

One such unit was my office, and it was a genuine printing company but with a lot of differences. First and foremost, I failed to understand in the first few months at the office that none of the Directors, seniors liked to call this company a printing unit. Positioning was more of a marketing company, professional enterprise branding, marketing print products, etc. We always wanted to position ourselves as experts, advisory, and leaders from the marketing industry. I underwent sales training that emphasized why we liked to be set like that.

One such day arrived when we met the Director who led Sales. There was a lot of hype created before his visit. How to arrive before you really arrive is something I learnt that day.

The Director walked in, and there was pin-drop silence. He glanced in the room and made eye contact with everyone sitting, and asked a question, "What do you think direct marketing is"? Someone in the room said; Direct marketing consists of any marketing that relies on direct communication or distribution to individual consumers rather than through a third party such as mass media. The next question followed, "And how do you sell?" This question appeared relatively simple to many people; everyone whispered that it means meeting people, explaining your product features, giving an offer, etc. The Director raised his hand, indicating all of us to stop talking. His expression was of dejection, the wrinkles on his forehead almost communicated we are a bunch of wrong salespeople appointed. Fortunately, he didn't lose hope in us and asked us another question "What do you think a doctor does when you visit him or her the first time"? Someone in the room said, we tell the doctor how we feel physically and mentally, our problems, our challenges, what failed home remedies we took, and seek his expert advice. That brought a broad smile to this face. What a relief it was for all!

He then explained that we need to be a consultant to be a good seller, just like a doctor. The patient (customer) needs to put faith in you as a doctor (seller), open up in front of you, seek your expertise and expect a solution from you. And, for this to happen, you need to be a great listener. He continued that if your customer does not find comfort while talking to you, he will not buy no matter the price, the features, and the offer you give. Your customer has to like you. He also explained the art of preparing for any meeting as ours was a B2B model dealing with senior Marketing people in the Corporates, Managing Directors, and Company Secretaries of large listed companies.

Though we were a bunch of young boys and girls in our twenties, we had to carry ourselves well in front of these senior buyers with proper time management, dressing up well, over-prepare (I have covered this later in this book), with effective written and oral communication that was vital to make sure the buyer starts liking you over a period of time. Finally, he also said, "you should arrive before you actually arrive at such meetings."

Selling print can be technical, but the art of selling anything is not to get technical. If only we can bring out the benefits of our products or services, the buyer will be happy to hear, especially if they are convinced it will make life easy, offer help, reduce their work, simplify their work, etc. Whatever reduces their effort at a reasonable price is acceptable. While most buyers claim to be more technical than what you are, never stop them from talking technical or arguing as they want to give you a message that we cannot fool them on specifications or terms. We need to know our technical side well and handle our customer. The customer has a challenge, and if you can get a grip on that, you can nail the deal.

The Cambridge Dictionary says a consultant is a person who is a specialist in a particular subject and whose job is to give advice and information to businesses, government organizations, etc. A successful consultant can provide the right direction from his experience and expertise to enable future growth and development to companies. The Harvard Business School provides a more specific definition of a consultant as someone who advises on "how to modify, proceed in, or streamline a given process within a specialized field."

In his book, *The Consulting Bible*, Alan Weiss defines that "When we [consultants] walk away from a client, the client's conditions should be better than it was before we arrived or we've failed." The message to us was loud and clear, make your customers feel very comfortable with your expertise and experience to further believe in the company's ability.

After my college days and the Management Institute I went to, this training day taught me many things. When the day ended, there was a feeling of "I have arrived." I thought of my father, who was no more there to hear the story of my eventful day. I felt his void as I missed those evenings when he used to return from work and patiently hear me tell him the events of the day.

I met my colleagues at this training as we were about ten people. A few experienced, having worked for organizations, but a few were freshers like me. Many of them became very dear friends over the years.
It was time to go home, and I saw myself squeezed in a packed local train for my journey back home from Lower Parel to Santacruz.

An activity you can do:

1. After your pitch to a new customer, as you leave the meeting, step into the shoes of your customer and think would you be happy to meet a person like you?
2. Would you be glad to hear about a product or service or a solution you just heard of?
3. Would you get satisfaction or a sense of enrichment that you have gained some knowledge and incredible insight?

4. Would you be empowered to make a decision you otherwise wouldn't have made had you not met a person like you? Where you successful in not giving away or hiding a feeling of selling from creeping in?

If you feel positive about these above thoughts, then you are on your path to being a good consultant, which will eventually make you a good seller, as your customers will trust you in the long run.

2. The power of effective communication – your most potent skill

We all know the power of effective communication. Is it plain how we talk, write, orate? No, it's not.

The word communication means *"to make common."* At its most basic level, it means letting your needs be known. At its highest level, communication means building strong, trusting relationships with people whose perspectives are very different from your own. The educator and psychotherapist Virginia Satir wrote, "Once a human being has arrived on this earth; communication is the largest single factor determining what kinds of relationships he makes with others and what happens to him in the world." It also determines whether you are capable of being a highly effective leader.

Communication is:

- Expressing yourself well
- Listening and responding timely
- Showing attention and right intention

Besides what and how you've understood, I learnt that if you can make someone else understand easily, that's more effective communication. If you cannot explain something complex in a simplified manner to someone else, first and foremost, you've not understood it well.

Once there was a meeting fixed with the then Managing Director of a leading paint company in India. We were a team of ten people called to meet the Managing Director (MD) at Nariman Point. Each had a role to play, and mine was the least important as someone who had joined recently. I accompanied the team more to observe and learn how a PowerPoint presentation is made to clients - the plan was to show various options the creative team had created for the client's Annual Report cover design.

The journey from our Worli office to Nariman Point that day was very different for me. Imagine a young boy, accompanying his new colleagues, sitting in the car with them discussing strategies, approach, who will lead, who will settle down first, who will make notes, who knows where all the samples are and when they are needed to be shown, etc. In all this, the senior members of the team were quiet, as if to test if all of us knew our roles. The car in which we sat was airconditioned. The usual chaos of Mumbai's traffic was not felt inside, and I was thoroughly enjoying every moment in my excitement.

The room was set, the technical connections were doubly checked to make sure the laptop works well, functions, and shows the right design at the right time. The speaker from our side was my Director, who went on to be my mentor. However, I never worked under him directly. Everything I learnt I had picked up by keenly observing this guru of mine. He wore a blazer without a tie and appeared straight from a large MNC. For a printing company to be represented in this manner was unheard of. The team, the way we were told to dress, the preparation for the meeting, the samples we carried etc., everything was planned to the last detail.
Even today, I'm learning from him.

The MD walked in and settled down after the initial greetings, and the presentation started.

Here was my observation:
- All in the room were making notes on what was said and spoken. Every pause during the meeting was noted. Every disturbance of the intercom ringing, the MD's reactions to slides presented, the designs showed, his questions, our answers etc., everything was getting noted.

In my opinion, the power of communication was most established when two girls from our team who worked very closely with our Director got a wild stare from him when one of them couldn't give him a sample of another Annual Report he was referring to during his talk.

- This silent communication was something I could notice very well.

- I also saw the Director talk with authority and confidence and display all the knowledge of the designs presented with the rationale and thought process behind each design.

- Then I also saw the power of effectively using one's hands and fingers. The way a sample was held and caressed was awe-inspiring and so convincing as if it was by far the best work we had ever produced.

As I mentioned earlier, print is a part of the technical industry, but it's all creative, design, paper, and finish, differentiating a product from good and great.

Finally, the time came to present the proposal. We were never told to send the bid, offer or quotation to clients through an office assistant or email it. If that was how it could be sent, why does the company need us? It was often discussed that as a Salesperson, do not lose any opportunity to meet your potential or new client, and a proposal was one of the most crucial stages to win or lose a deal.

I could see how my Director's fingers held the proposal. It was not folded and slipped into an envelope, but it was out as if a top-secret was being revealed; the excitement and pause were all part of the communication. The Director held the opaque plastic folder in which the proposal was filed neatly signed by him. He went on to talk about other things till the curiosity reached its peak, and finally, the MD said, "I'm keen to see your commercial terms as I've liked the designs you've presented today; the effort is commendable." Suddenly I could see a sigh of relief amongst all our team members. There were smiles on our faces as we knew the pricing would not be the deciding factor as the client was already "sold" on other aspects. Believe me, the designs were not simple to understand as it was for a paint company, unlike a consumer goods or a pharma company in which the creation becomes relatively more straightforward. The rationale had to be explained well to appeal to the MD and relate to the brief given. What I saw and heard that day was my team's power of effective communication.

It was altogether a different feeling on our way back. We were all excited; there was a lot of talk on what went right, what could have gone wrong, the humour, the jokes, and all in all, how we got this big and prestigious project. It was a project worth twenty-five lacs Indian rupees, quite a considerable sum in the nineties.

This first meeting with the client had a lasting impact on me. Lessons on the real power of communication.

An activity you can do:

Do the below, which I have done in the past to improve my communication skills:

- Read a paragraph from a book loudly every day to practice your oral communications.
- Talk looking into a mirror and observe yourself - body language, tone of voice, clarity and confidence in your speech.

3. No shortcuts, however urgent.

Just as we were settling down in our new company and the training was almost ending, a crucial session was scheduled. At first, it appeared pretty simple when we read about it "how to prepare." Yes, it was just that, I remember distinctly.

By now, we all talked to each other very freely, and the experienced team members were always more talkative and put their weight on us more than the others.

I asked an experienced colleague about this "how to prepare" session and the reason why it was so important. Anoop was the Executive I remember, neatly dressed, wore a tie from day one and was a confident fellow. He said, "Remember, every company has its way of handling things from customer query, finalizing the deal till execution and once you know this, it becomes easy." Sounded perfect to me.

This session started, and the first thing on the board was "how not to handle a sales call"? It was a radically different approach about what mustn't be done rather than explaining what must be done. Brilliant. Negative things tend to enter our minds faster than straightforward things.

From the standard operating procedures, the specifications we needed to ask our customer to offer them a price, the schedule of execution, i.e., how a date plan is prepared from receipt of data and material from client to making a prototype, procurement of critical components like paper, production and binding schedule to the despatch plan, everything was explained to us systematically. Most importantly, the reason why we need to know was explained.

This session made me rich in knowing the crucial steps of execution, and all that we had in the last few days was making a lot of sense now. None of us were from the printing, media, advertising or publishing background, but now we could relate with print and its execution model very well.

Further, we learnt the importance of preparing for a meeting with our clients and how to go about it. Broadly the steps were (remember those were the pre-Google days):

Here are few things we learnt:

- Try to get to know everything about the customer's company from whatever sources you can, that was the first lesson – pick up print material from the customer's reception area, newsletters, diaries, annual reports, calendars, etc.

- Find out who is their Advertising agency to get a head-start somewhere if we've worked with them earlier.

- Ask seniors in your own company if by any chance they know the customer you are planning to meet.

Then it was time to learn to prepare our sales kit. Simple as it may appear, but the speaker insisted, "Do not go for any meeting without these in your bag":

- Samples of your work – carry the ones more relevant to your meeting
- Calculator
- Scale
- Paper sample swatches
- Notepad
- Diary

- Carry a Case Study in your mind that you have successfully handled, which your customer will be happy to know. Grab the first opportunity to narrate this Case Study if the customer shows interest.

Even today, you will find the above items in my bag.

The training didn't end there. It was time to discuss some finer points, namely:

- Reach ten minutes before time.

- Settle down, use the washroom, carry a deodorant, wash and clean your hands.

- Smile and leave all your thoughts outside the reception area and focus.

- Remember, you have the crucial first one minute to impress.

- Shake hands with your customer firmly if it's a male and gently if it's a lady.

- Always wait till the customer speaks first as you need their attention. If there's any disturbance, wait, allow time for the phone calls in between, or if the customer is in the midst of something, let them finish their work.
- Ask them how much time they have with you. When you ask this question, it indicates that you mean business and would not want theirs and your time wasted. The customer takes you seriously when you ask this.

- Do not say no to a coffee or a tea offered. The more time you get with your customer, the better it is.

- Look around the customer's desk, walls, etc. It gives a glimpse into the customer's character, his taste, liking and choice.

- Be attentive to know where the customer's interest could be – weather, traffic, cricket, movies, songs, jokes, books, magazines etc. You then learn how to develop a relationship with them later. You know which topic to discuss every time you meet.

A vital lesson was the concept of "adding value." When a product or service is made more appealing, customers will usually pay more. Therefore, adding value increases the profit that a business can make. Remember, adding value gets you attention, engagement and of course premium also.

In this hyper-competitive world, where there's little differentiation, how do you grab the attention of your potential customer? Price, Quality, Service, Delivery are not the differentiators to win you deals anymore; they are given and presumed to be in place. Can you offer the most competitive price and produce a shabby product? Can you provide excellent quality and go wrong with service? Can you do everything right and be late in delivery? Of course not.

The customer looks for something else. The customer has to first like you, engage with you, see you as a professional and then if all the competitive parameters are in place, you have a solid case to win the deal. To add value can be the way you carry yourself, the unexpected benefit you offer beyond promises made, your professional time-bound approach, your advisory behaviour or your approach to customer's interest.

When you do all this, the customer will not look at the competition or will at least revert to you on your pricing if it's on the higher side or give you the feedback you are looking for. Getting into a situation where the customer is keener to work with you will always be beneficial in the long term. We were told to lose battles but were groomed to win wars in the long term.

These lessons were like gold dust which I treasure to date. This approach is what I've carried with me even today, and I put it into practice whenever I can. It's almost instinctive and expected today to want things to be easier, faster, and better. But shortcuts don't guarantee success. When we take shortcuts, we tend to be careless and emphasize speed rather than quality.

Can you imagine the risk of shortcuts in food safety practices? Can you imagine a maintenance engineer treating a broken nut casually during routine check-ups of a Jumbo airliner? Think about it.

Activity for you:

Here again, no matter what stage of your career you are in. Don't worry thinking you don't make sales calls anymore (which itself is a problem in any case) but try and answer the below questions:

1. Are you Sales equipped at any given point in time?

2. Do you have your updated tools of communications you can send to your potential customer from your phone or laptop at any given point in time?
3. Do you carry your physical tools every time you step out to meet your customers? You may not get them out of your bag but are you Sales ready?
4. How much time do you spend preparing for a meeting fixed in advance?
5. Do you practice sending regular Minutes, action sheets to your customers after the meeting and following up?
6. Most importantly, do you think of creative ways to stay in touch with your potential customers than just following up in the usual boring manner?

4. Lateral Thinking

It took me over a year to realize after starting my career with this company. By now, all my colleagues who had joined at the same time were very comfortable with eachother, celebrating each other's success, teaching and helping when someone went wrong or needed help, and as a team, we were bonding well.

This repeated help to eachother triggered this thought in my mind.

How and why was I selected? I had no background in the printing industry, I had never worked for any company in the past, not done any education in print, graphic or media, and despite that, I was here selling print products. On further introspection, I realized that none of the ten people who started with me had any background in print. As mentioned, few were experienced, and most of us were freshers, but those who had worked for someone else were also not from the print industry. All this appeared incredible to me.

My curiosity grew when I looked around, and to my surprise, I also found that most of the staff connected to sales, marketing, customer service was not from the print industry. The ones who had a thorough knowledge of the graphics and the print side were in the pre-press stage, including design, creative, DTP, the people on the shop floor, and the production executive staff, including supervisors and co-ordinators between sales and production.

I finally understood why we were taught not to position ourselves as printers. Had I asked this question to anyone in the training sessions, I'm sure no one would have answered it correctly. It had taken that self-realization which in a way confirms the belief. The reason was that the company always wanted to position itself as a "marketing" company, and printed products were an extension of this thought process. I was convinced that we wouldn't have called ourselves Bakers or a Cake Shop if we were selling cakes. We wouldn't be known as people in garments if we were in clothing.

This thought may confuse or perplex many readers, but the idea was quite profound than what one can understand. It was way ahead of its time. Many have unknowingly practiced the concept of "lateral thinking" or "jugaad" for ages. In the last decade or so, it has been recognized as a serious model of thinking and execution; let's accept that. This hiring of salespeople from a non-print industry was nothing but a kind of jugaad or lateral thinking act, which worked brilliantly. We didn't carry any past baggage, nor did we have any preconceived notions of industry practices and used to challenge and accept things the way they were. While the competition was eyeing each other's people, hiring from traditional methods and getting similar results, this act of bringing different people from different mindsets applying sales techniques of various industries and the approach towards freshers like us was yielding great results.

How many companies do you know who do not deliberately hire people from their industry? How many would insist on not having this in their selection criteria? Would a solar product manufacturer say we don't want anyone selling solar products? Would a company from the construction & building industry mention in their job profile sheet for hiring salespeople they don't need anyone from the architects, building, construction industry?

This thought process was a radically different approach.

I tried implementing this strategy in the latter half of my career when I started interviewing and hiring people. The reasons this strategy did work were as follows:

- Fresh minds are easy to shape as they do not carry any baggage. They do not know competitors to compare and mess up their careers by comparing working culture, infrastructure, competitiveness, facilities, etc. They accept as things are and adapt.

- People work for people, not for the companies hiring them. If the interviewer can inspire the interviewee with the company's plans, growth models, show how all can grow together, excite the new employee on what's in store and implement progressively, attrition can be arrested even if the pay scale is not very appealing.

- Work culture, once it stands out in people's minds, even for a considerable hike, a person would think many times before switching jobs.

- Most notably, a person from a different background and industry experience gets a fresh perspective in performance. He doesn't carry the industry's usual practices, which sometimes can prove to be masterstrokes.

While a school of thought may argue that hiring from different industry backgrounds can be a risk as things can go very wrong, customers would know that quickly and make the person and the company employing the same appear very foolish. Over the years, I felt the advantages outweigh the disadvantages. Let me give you an example.

There was a girl in our team by the name of Cathy. She worked in the travel industry and was good-looking, very confident, and excellent in written and oral communications. She was hired with an apparent objective to get a foot in the door with the right clients and set a platform for the team to do the rest. After all the training sessions, I had realized that she had not picked up the technical side of our industry, but when it came to fixing appointments, going for those first meetings and breaking the ice, she was outstanding.

On one late evening, Cathy walked into the office with me and a few others around as we were about to call our day off, and she gave me a brief on how her day had gone by. As the conversation went on, I could sense we were in for some trouble, I could sense she had over-committed to a project, and we would have to turn the tables upside down to make things happen.

Cathy had accepted a project to print, bind and deliver over a dozen print products and had agreed to provide everything the next day before nine in the morning. It was an event scheduled with top delegates from the Government who were to attend the event. Their existing printer had goofed up and had raised his hands, and the company was desperate to find an alternative at this last hour. Cathy had accepted it, not knowing the repercussion of this project's stress, but somewhere I could understand her mindset also.

It was a near-impossible situation, but we could do it. No one from my team, including me, went home that night. The entire sales, back-end and production staff worked till seven in the morning, and the delivery van left to deliver well before the morning's nine o'clock deadline.

Keep thinking about what could have happened had we not delivered - penalties, disaster in the market, losing that client forever, etc. Everything was possible, but that taught me something. What would a person from the print industry do when the client chose to give this project to us at that hour, as accepted by Cathy the other day. This person would have evaluated the possibilities, the time needed and the time we had, the problems, the challenges etc. and would have probably rejected the project. It was the easiest thing to do. Sometimes ignorance is bliss, as they say. The culture built-in the company helped us to stand by Cathy. We all raised to the occasion and backed ourselves with the available resources, and could deliver what appeared impossible prima-facie.

When competition is tough, product differentiation is negligible; a customer is spoilt for options; these are the moments that we need to grab to build a relationship with clients that lasts for a long time. Cathy became the best salesperson that quarter, she thanked everyone, and we all celebrated her success. The client became one of our top clients in revenue and profits. Even after years, when Cathy left the organization as she got married and moved on to a different city, the client remained with us.

Activity for you:

1. What jugaad ways have you tried for your business - Jugaad in hiring, product development, networking etc.
2. Can you experiment by hiring someone not from your industry asking how they would sell your product or service? You will be surprised to get the feedback. Try it.

3. Books you may like to read:

- Lateral Thinking by Edward de Bono
- Thinking Fast and Slow by Daniel Kahneman

5. The power of Presentations

Going for a sales pitch with the team always excited me. In the initial days, it appeared another day in the office when we used to plan for our meetings but then a day arrived. I distinctly remember it was for a tea plantation company. My fascination and liking for PowerPoint presentations started then. It became one of my most powerful tools in every meeting I attended, be it for sales, marketing, research presentation, and data analysis. Still, before I continue further on that, let's understand something more on these PowerPoint presentations.

Microsoft PowerPoint is a presentation program created by Robert Gaskins and Dennis Austin at Forethought, Inc. It was released on April 20, 1987, initially for Macintosh computers only. Microsoft acquired PowerPoint for about $14 million three months after it appeared (source: Wikipedia). The purpose of PowerPoint is to act as a visual aid as a presenter presents their option, ideas, sales pitch, etc.

Simple rules for better PowerPoint presentations I follow:

- Don't read your presentation straight from the slides.
- Don't forget your audience.
- Choose readable colors and fonts.
- Don't overload your presentation with animations.
- Use animations sparingly to enhance your presentation.

Broadly here are the advantages of using a PowerPoint presentation:

- It can be used virtually anywhere, both professionally and personally also.
- It is a collaborative tool excellent for pooling in with your team members.
- There are various templates, or you can simply create your formats.
- It can be used for social media posts creation, flyers, posters, videos etc. An excellent multi-usage tool indeed.
- It can be exported to other formats: pdf, mp4, gifs, png, or jpeg.

It can sometimes also give you specific challenges, and a few disadvantages are:

- Can cause technical issues which you have not anticipated.
- People tend to get carried away and load it with content so much that it can give you a nightmare to format everything in order.
- Your over dependence on slides can take the essence of the point you are trying to make, making the audience read them more than listening to you.
- Over a while, over-usage can cause more harm to your presentations as the audience often switches off listening to you as they know you will only use the slides to make a point.

The advantages outweigh the disadvantages as it's proven that 89% of people use PowerPoint presentations.

****

A tea plantation company was my client, and we all got together to put our best foot forward as it was with the Managing Director of the company who wanted to see the Annual Report cover designs.

The team could create a ten-slide presentation starting from a format that became a template for all of us. The flow was as follows:

- A brief on the Company - It's vital highlights of the year gone by and some key indicators such as profits made, sales, new markets they had entered etc.

This opening set the tone for the company to see a good amount of research was done, and a feel-good factor sets in with the audience as they relate immediately.

- The company always gave a brief to us on what they expected on the cover.

The brief is one of the most crucial slides as it has to be very accurate or can just derail the entire meeting. Imagine the person who had given the brief denying the brief or even mentioning, "I didn't mean this." This error can prove costly and takes us back to the person who brought the brief, the understanding behind it, getting both on the same page, re-confirming on an email to ensure all are on track–the brief, when precise, helps in creating many options.

- Then comes a rationale - what have we thought about the brief given to us. Here, we get the opportunity to express and show the client the thought process gone behind the kind of work, research, and analysis we've got into. I noticed our speaker took a lot of time on this slide, making sure everyone in the audience nodded affirmatively. Once this is done, trust me, the following slides, which have the actual designs become easy to sell. Half of the work is achieved when you see this affirmation. It's like the audience starts talking amongst themselves and has already decided that we are on track and the designs they will see will be correct. But I could see our speaker did not rush to move on to the actual design slides. The slide with the rationale was up on the board, and I think everyone must have read it at least thrice, making sure we nail this completely. A valuable lesson learnt.

- Then came the three designs we presented, one after the other. On an average, we spent ten minutes explaining the colors used; the logo positioned, the fonts and images used, the theme thought of, etc. etc. - all of which were spot on with the brief and the rationale on which we had spent so much time.

Not surprisingly, we got approval on one of the designs, and we won that deal. It was an INR ten lacs order but not before

I found out later something very interesting. No one knew this, but the designs presented all had a strategy behind them. Out of the three designs, one was the best, and all had put their money on it internally from our side. There was another one that had earned a second shortlist in our minds, and the last one was made to ensure the client gets the satisfaction of rejecting it on the face of it. It was an outstanding lesson learnt again. Clients have an ego and always want to say and behave as if they know more than us, whether creatives, designs, analysis, actions, etc. The idea was to satisfy their ego and say they didn't like the third one so that the entire focus goes on the first two designs. The moment we realized the client was getting hooked to the other two, putting more pressure to get that final affirmation was easy.

Well, this doesn't get over here. At the end of the meeting, with all smiles around, we noticed another gentleman sitting in a corner who was the Managing Director's friend. He had joined in without our notice to see this presentation. To our surprise, he was later introduced to us, and we learnt he was also an owner of a pharma company. He was already sold with what he had seen and said that he also wanted us to work on designs for his own company. It was a windfall happening right there in front of my eyes.

An Activity you can do:

If you are from the creative, advertising, marketing, social media agency side etc., the above is an excellent example to get inspired.

But if you are from another industry and rely on presenting PowerPoint presentations in your client meetings, here's what you can do:

1. Keep them simple
2. They can access all your company credentials from your website, so don't bother putting them on the slide except having the website address at the end.
3. Navigate their thought process - make them think in a direction you want them to. It could be in terms of an offer they cannot refuse, a package to choose from, a solution to their most significant pain area etc.
4. Practice the content well and do not rely on the slides. There are many access points - keep the slides ready on all your devices.
5. Finally, remember the hook. The audience should connect with your thought and the brief they had given you.

6. It's all about passion

Our peak sales season was from March to Sept. As the financial year ended, as printers of Annual Reports, we used to keenly follow the year closure dates of Corporates and calculate the last day companies can hold their Annual General Meeting (AGM). Majorly, the companies had a March-ending financial year, and the last date to hold their AGM was thirtieth September.

As a part of the front-end sales team, we were given a list of new clients to get new business and service the existing clients we had from last year to ensure repeat business. The team meetings in the last week of March focused on forecasting - the probability of sales each Executive can get from their existing client base. The predictability was based on confidence, how we serviced and performed last year to get that gut feeling if the sales can be repeated with a ten percent escalation in the invoice value. This prediction was not tricky, though not very easy too. Competitors were always eyeing our customer list, and the good price would always tilt the balance adversely. Still, I learnt that despite high prices in few cases, the customer favoured us, which made me curious. One such client was the paint giant Asian Paints, personally serviced by our director, who had something in him that brought us business repeatedly over the years. The keyword was the relationship. I had never seen the kind of rapport and bond with a customer, especially in B2B sales. Our prices were always high, and every year we used to get a final goal post to match, which would not have been possible without the kind of relationship we had with the client there. He was one of our top clients, and he was looked after well. The servicing was consistently proactive; the treatment when the client visited our premises for the DTP work, designing, proofing, etc., was personalized. Most importantly, we used to get advance payment from the client on demand which was quite phenomenal. All this happened under personal supervision of this director.

Let me give the reader a glimpse of the Annual Report printing work we used to do for the Corporates. As mentioned earlier, every listed company on the Bombay Stock Exchange (BSE) needs to publish, print and send an Annual Report copy to its shareholder within six months of its financial year's closure date. Ninety percent of listed companies on the BSE had to complete this before September ended. Still, few had different year endings, namely, September and December and accordingly, their six months used to finish ahead. As a printing firm, we were busy from March to September the most, but there was that ten percent focus also later. Companies now have the option to send a PDF version of the Annual Report approved by the Companies Act and SEBI, but before this, Annual Report printing was a central focus area for printing firms. Companies printed a shareholder version sent to all shareholders with limited content and a deluxe premium version using high-quality paper, more colourful, graphical representation of data etc. We were trained on every aspect of the Annual Report content, so much so that we knew which schedule of data needs to come on which page of the Annual Report, the legal provisions, the mailing dates, the printing priority, etc.

My first boss was Mr. Mukesh Dhruve, Director, Repro India Limited, a Chartered Accountant who led this sales team. It was a fantastic model created, taught and trained by a CA. As sales executives, we met the Company Secretaries of listed companies who were our direct target since they used to be instrumental in deciding with whom they would print the Annual Report. It was high-end relationship marketing that we learnt and our confidence, capabilities, knowledge and print firm's credibility, was what which used to work. There was a stark difference in us vis-à-vis our competitors in every aspect. The only place they could beat us was the price, and we had to build a relationship and engaging experience, after which clients used to get hooked on to us. This Annual Report product marketing allowed me to meet senior people in listed companies - from Company Secretaries, Design team, PR departments to even Managing Directors and

Chairmen of these companies. For them, this was a very serious product, and a lot of importance and attention was given to this product. Annual Report as a product was the face of the company and a communication tool which went to its shareholders once a year. Over the years, I introduced and developed clients such as the ICICI Group, IDBI Bank, Tata Group, Torrent Group, Nirma, Hindustan Lever to many top clients. This product allowed me to meet Mr. Ratan Tata, Mr. Narayan Murthy, and Mr. K. V. Kamath, who personally took an interest in their Annual Report printing.

In one such peak season of our Annual Report printing, we printed one shareholder version of it for a small company that was in the pharmaceutical industry. It was my client, and I was keen to see how it looked as it was just out of the press and, as usual, was sent to my director's cabin before reaching us. It was a late evening, but the office was busy as usual as many clients used to sit with our design and DTP team to complete the typesetting and proofing work. I was at my desk when my intercom rang. My director was on the line, and he called me to his cabin with urgency. The first thought in my mind was, "Ghosh, there would be a mistake somewhere, and now that all copies are printed, it would be irreparable." The walk from the desk to his cabin was one of the longest that day. I was already thinking of working on some solution and how to handle it. Bravely, I entered his place, and to my bad luck, there were few more people in his cabin. I thought I would get shouting in front of everyone, which would be more embarrassing. But guess what happened?

My director looked at me and said, "Come Rajnish, just look at this copy which has just come." My curiosity grew further, but I was unsure what was coming ahead. I asked him, "how it is, Sir." He held the copy in front of me just like how you would hold a baby in your hand. He then caressed it, smelled the paper, flipped the cover page gently and then the rest of the pages and said, "look at this neat job done, the pages look so good, the print on this paper we used is so bright and the graphs despite being in one color look so attractive. You serviced this client so well, and that reflects in this copy also". I was amazed and bemused for a moment. With great difficulty, I smiled at him and said thank you.

I went out of the cabin, obviously relieved and sat in one corner wondering what happened. I stared at the copy repeatedly, wondering what on earth was so good in it. In technical terms, it was a forty-eight-page copy, printed in one blue color and was center stapled. I couldn't see the beauty my director noticed, but I was keen to know further.

Such incidents were very frequent and finally, I understood in one word what it was; what the director expressed was nothing but passion. It was the love for the product, the result of the hard work, and nothing short of the happiness and joy one gets when one sees a new born baby. It was nothing but pure passion.

Over these twenty-five years of my experience and after reading many books on sales and marketing, I'm convinced that the below work the best to be successful in sales:

- Prospecting rightly
- Knowing your customers well
- Possessing sound written and oral communication skills
- Storytelling abilities
- Engaging with customers
- Relationship building
- Consulting and not Selling
- Offering value propositions
- Being very pro-active, concerned and always putting customer's interests ahead
- Having a research-oriented mind
- Being well-read and informed on your respective industry, your customer's industry and the trends. Know from where the wind is blowing.
- Networking in the right places
- Adapting to situations
- Have deep hunger to learn.
- Doing all this with exceeding passion and commitment consistently. The ability to see through the process from prospecting to winning the deal to making sure the product or service is delivered as promised. Nothing is more pleasing than experiencing this.

An activity you can do:

How do you know where your passion lies?

Try answer these questions:

1. Which part of the work do you do which doesn't stress you? Don't just say Sales generally as an example - dig deep into it. Is it the customer acquisition part from preparation to meeting them or the follow-up part? Some people are great ice-breakers, they get the foot in the door, and others would need the platform to be created, and then they take off from there.

   In short, are you a farmer or a hunter?
2. Look for high points in your day which you enjoy.
3. Think about your strengths.

Entrepreneur and investor Sam Altman says some of the best advice he ever received was, "If you can't figure out what kind of work you like, pay attention to what's easy to concentrate on and gives you energy vs. what makes you tune out and feel tired."

What is easy for you to concentrate on?

7. Always have a role model for yourself

My story relates to the epic Mahabharata with the character called *Eklavya.* Just like how *Dronacharya* never taught *Eklavya* directly, I, too, never was groomed or directly managed by my role model or my mentor. What I learnt was through observation and just by listening to him.

It was my first ever sales review meeting way back when I started my career, and we were a bunch of trainees and sales executives sitting in the conference room with a notebook in our hands. Honestly, way back, we all were clueless about what the meeting was all about but were aware it would be an evaluation of the week gone by. Imagine for someone like me who had never worked previously, no connection of corporate culture of any kind, someone who had never planned sales as a career sitting in the conference room. It was too overwhelming for all of us. The room was chilled as the air-conditioner was at its best, almost freezing us there, but no one dared to say that. It was a long wait, and the delay only worsened things. Finally, my role model, my mentor, Dushyant Mehta, entered with a bunch of his team members in the conference room. Dushyant is a tall dark man with a magnetic personality and carries himself with utmost confidence. His body language is by far the best I've seen, making the person sitting in front of him look like dwarfs and timid.

I realized why he is my mentor only after I left the company where we had met. His practices, thinking and approach, got into me so much that I realized it later, not when we were together. A role model inspires you, motivates you to raise your bar, almost makes you imitate him to act and do everything he does, and unknowingly that happened with me over these years.

Here are a few of my stories with Dushyant:

I worked in surroundings and in a culture in the initial part of my career, which was very haphazard and unstructured. Everything was planned at the last minute; there were surprises at every execution stage, which frustrated us. In one of the meetings, Dushyant tried to explain how to do you participate thoroughly and anticipate what the other will require from you pro-actively. He used to say, "Follow-up is the biggest industry in the world." This sentence got stuck in my mind. Indeed, the most prominent industry has to be "follow-up," not steel, IT, Chemicals, Banking etc. Everybody loves follow-up, may it be for any industry. People will not do their job correctly, putting pressure on others who need to follow up with them. Test this even in your day-to-day life, and you will realize this. My key takeaway was how to make sure no one follow-ups with me. He used to say the chain of good performance is long - make sure you at least don't break the rhythm.

****

Crisis in the print industry is very typical. It's a way of life, and when everything used to flow smoothly, we used to get edgy and restless. One fine day, as usual, there was some issue that was much bigger and irreparable because everyone from front-end executives, the design team, production to the Management team were all in the conference room to handle it. After understanding the whole situation, Dushyant asked the person who had noticed the issue and what he did first when he found the mistake. The person replied that he panicked and rushed to the managing director to narrate everything. Everyone thought that was the right thing to do, but Dushyant said something surprising. He said, "that's the easiest thing to do." After noticing the mistake, he meant that briefing the managing director on the issue was easiest. Passing the buck moving the pressure from one head to the other doesn't solve the problem. Yes, I do not deny that informing the superiors is not the right thing, but going to them with possible solutions can also help. This approach was an excellent lesson to grab again, reflecting an attitude.

Are you a problem announcer only or someone who also gives solutions?

****

Every time there was a small event, a celebration party in the company, Dushyant mentioned the three stages. I wondered what those three stages were until I finally understood when we were planning another event.

The three stages were pre-event, event and post-event activities. He always insisted on breaking any task into these three stages, which simplified things. Try this even for a small birthday party you may hold in your house, and you will understand further.

The next time you are anchoring or even part of an event, a big task in hand, try doing this. Simply break the task into these three stages and focus on each activity one by one. You will be amazed to see the results and how your stress reduces.

****

An event organized by the Public Relations Society of India (PRSI) was held at The Taj Hotel in Mumbai, and my company had partly sponsored it. The idea to fund was because it would be attended by very senior people from companies, managing directors and the PR and Marketing Heads of top companies. When general networking was happening during dinner time, Dushyant approached me and told me to somehow meet and exchange my visiting card with the Head of Public Relations of Tata Steel. His name was Milind Rege, a well-known person as he was also the ex-Captain of the Mumbai Cricket Team. He played a significant role in allotting print business to vendors with the Annual Report print project valuing around a crore Indian Rupees then. It was also a prestigious print product even we were eyeing. My director Dushyant motivated me enough to say that if we can get an entry into the Tata Group through Tata Steel, doors would open for us with other group companies. I dared to look into Milind Rege's eyes and walked into him to introduce myself on my own. I could do this because cricket was common between Milind Rege and me. When I told him I'd played cricket for my college and for the Mumbai under seventeen age group and Anna Vaidya was my coach at Shivaji Park, that was enough for him to notice me. I remember I could break the ice with ease. We went on to talk about cricket for a while before he excused, not before telling me to come and meet me at the office. I was thrilled, and so was Dushyant. Later, I learnt that Dushyant knew Milind very well but didn't want to approach him directly to ask for the print business. Dushyant, on his own, probably, wouldn't have pursued meetings after that, something that was expected from me. Over the years, I developed excellent relations at Tata Steel, Tata Chemicals, Tata Tea and TCS. I was told few years down the line that cumulatively, we did a business of over fifty crores with The Tata Group over ten-year period. That was the power of that one meeting.

This prospecting and sowing seeds for eyeing long-term vital accounts is an excellent lesson for anyone wanting to develop long-term relationships. If you sense a client's potential is enormous, a systematic approach, building relations slowly proves to be the foundation. You should believe in the potential, should be motivated enough and be persistent. The Tata Group example is a significant success story in my life. It was a time when Ratan Tata had taken over as their leader and had already declared that all group companies would now have to work on merits and would not favour eachother for businesses to move within the group only. Despite the group having Tata Press, our competitor, this announcement created the platform for us to be ambitious and approach their biggest company. It is crucial to be alert with what is happening with companies, your target groups, their decisions, the policy changes, etc. All this impacts your business, and only the smart can notice it and capitalize at the right time.

****

After the Annual Report printing season used to get over around September, we would then work on the print projects of Calendars and Diaries. We were working on one such calendar for Credit Suisse - an investment banker. This client was incidentally developed by a team member in the initial days, but somehow, we couldn't close the deal until Dushyant made a masterstroke one day.

In one of the final review meetings with all done for the Calendar season, this client's name popped up, and it was pretty embarrassing for my executive and me to answer why things were stuck for so long. The design was approved, the images were approved for all twelve months, but their Managing Director was not getting time to sign on the order for us to proceed as he was traveling, and it was not a priority for them. The Marketing Head with whom we were interacting was very defensive though very supportive to us. He couldn't go to his director for approvals and remind him repeatedly. This was quite a situation where the client liked everything but couldn't proceed. Dushyant told us to proof the entire calendar and meet the Marketing Head with it. One printed proof of the calendar was made, and we rushed to him. He was delighted to see the proof and quickly ran to his MD, fortunately, he was present in the office. Instead of only reminding the MD to sign on the work order, he had something to show this time. The MD signed on it as he also liked the proof, and it was all done in a few minutes.

A lesson learnt on how to close a deal. Another classic case of how a salesperson should not give up on his efforts. The results may not come instantly, sometimes even after doing everything right, but one needs to look at and explore what can help you tilt the order in your favour. In the above case, the proofing of the calendar worked. The next time you come in such situations, take a pause and think about what you can do but don't give up easily.

****

Every day with Dushyant was a learning day for me. The time spent with him was very precious, and I would observe him every time. The time he used to spend on strategic things, the bonding he had with his immediate team members, the humour he carried so well, and so was the case of his terror. Primarily, his anger was when tasks were not done with a hundred percent effort, deadlines not been met after consensus, and he hated ordinary work. I also observed time management; he was very particular and ensured everyone was aligned.

I remember a day late in his office when we were very casually discussing "what if" scenarios with the way our business can be taken ahead. The resources then were very scarce - capital, people and infrastructure. With the "what if" scenario, we could brainstorm on revenues, new client acquisition, repeat business model, limitations, the areas where we can get hit, industry trends, challenges, tech impact and where our plans can go wrong. I was lucky to be a part of this brainstorming. To my utter surprise, at the end of the one-hour brainstorm, he looked at me and said, "Rajnish, our strategic plan is ready for next year now. Thank you for your inputs, you were terrific today, and I appreciate your thinking and reading of our business". This statement was gold dust to me, the words still ring in my mind, and it gives me goosebumps even now. His belief in me helped me shape my career to a great extent. Even today, I think of situations how he would think and act - in times of strategic actions, marketing and sales. I was fortunate to have a person like Dushyant in my life who could shape me up. It was he who first spoke to me on the lateral thinking model. I was highly impressed with this model of thinking. It means solving problems by an indirect and creative approach, typically viewing the issue in a new and unusual light. The concept of jugaad may have come in recent times, but this innovative approach is what drives you to jugaad ways.

****

I also need to mention Mukesh Dhruve, a Chartered Accountant by qualification but the one who led the Annual Report print division in which I was one of the sales executives under him. One way to look at it was because the company when I joined was small, the reporting was direct to him, and I learnt a lot from him. An absolute street-smart seller, if I can put it. He knew where to hit and where it mattered the most. Identifying the pain areas early in conversations with clients, thinking on his feet, and having very high-level organizational skills were his strengths. I have sometimes seen him think so far ahead that the most challenging tasks in hand would appear "done" with no challenges around. In his typical Guajarati and Hindi mix of spoken English, he was a man many in the company would open up to vis-a-vis with the other

Directors. Multi-tasking came very easily to him. He also used to lead the company's finance and accounts department because of his qualification—this overall mix of traits always fascinated and inspired me.

What also connected me with him was his love for cricket, which I am equally fond of. He used to watch and even play the game. The company had a team, and we also practiced at the Club grounds. There was never a dull day in his company.

****

Another gentleman who deeply impacted me is Pramod Khera, another Director I reported in at the latter stages of my career before I ventured on my own. His background was in the IT industry.

He came into my life when I professionally faced one of my most difficult times. Imagine leading a not-needed vertical as it was increasingly more apparent to the management that servicing the developed markets was not their cup of tea due to expected infrastructural and quality performance standards. No one told me what was expected from me, but we performed as a team against all odds. From an eighty lacs Indian Rupees turnover, in about three years, I led a team to take the turnover to about seventeen crores from markets such as the UK, US and parts of Europe, but the writing on the wall was clear.

This performance was also when the company was undergoing a transformation in operations, technology adaptation, quality, sales verticals, etc. That is when Pramod Khera joined. When I think about it now, it was a happy coincidence and a last effort to set the structure in place with clarity in the markets we wanted to focus on. So, I got that breather to perform with the management support in the form of Pramod Khera, and I thoroughly enjoyed that period.

I saw him transform and then lead an unstructured corporate set-up, earlier enveloped by past glories, favouritism, to taking it to a culture of meritocracy. His silence spoke a lot, and then the way he took centre stage and led those meetings was phenomenal and inspiring. For the first time, professionalism and meritocracy, the words he introduced there, I was seeing were getting practiced. As a leader, he was terrific. He used to back me up and leave strategic decision making to me for my markets.

When I was about to leave for the UK once for my business development, I distinctly remember when he called me and gave me a long list of topics to report upon. He wanted me to write to him on strategy, market pulse, do a SWOT analysis, etc. I had submitted my report sitting late in London after the day's appointments were over and had thoroughly enjoyed working on it. For the first time, I felt someone was listening.

On my return to India, I got feedback from none other than my managing director that he had asked all Business Heads on their respective markets to report on something similarly, and he found my submission the best amongst all. How pleased I was, I remember. These are moments that stay with you and inspire you forever.

An activity you can do:

Find a mentor or a role model for yourself. They could be your parents, your neighbour, a relative, someone at the office like in my case. Trust me; it's not that they do not have flaws or that they do not go wrong, who don't as we all are humans and are bound to make mistakes, it's obvious but take inspiration from what they do good, absorb and implement the good things and ignore everything else.

Just list down names of people who inspire you.

8. The PSPD concept

This jargon was learnt from one session conducted by a Merchant Banker who said that they, investors, always like to see this PSPD in any potential company. In the PSPD, the P - stands for Profitability, S - stands for Scalability, P - for Predictability and D - for De-risking.

Simply brilliant when I think about it again and again. This has gone a long way in my thinking and shaped my entrepreneurial venture. From a top corporate to a micro-business model, having this concept into your thinking pattern can help you scale your business for sure. Eventually, you have to generate profits. It cannot always be a case of survival or "giving back to society." Even to do that, you will need money to be generated from your business to give back. I know many who started a business venture because they saw the initial spark; the buyers were ready to buy their product or service but couldn't see the scale after that. If businesses are not scalable, they will lose in the long-run. It's steam sooner or later will die off as sustainability will be challenged. By predictability, we want to be in businesses where we can see a forecastable model, something you can be sure to run the show. When even that is not seen, it becomes a big problem. How will you convince your investors if you cannot predict your business revenue?

Finally, the good old thought of spreading your risks. No matter which industry or business model you have, it's always good to have shock absorbers in your business, and that is where the de-risking comes in. The business environment can change overnight. Policies can be amended, competition can play its part, disruption in your industry can happen rapidly, everything around can change before you can anticipate, and your sole revenue model can be put to stress. At such times the other verticals work for you. You can either have a supplementary vertical supporting your core business or get into something unrelated. E.g., as a Car dealer, your core remains of selling cars but introducing insurance for the vehicles or selling accessories can be an alternative. An HR firm can stick to its core of consulting companies in HR policy making, labour management, etc., can start a training and development vertical or even add HR as an outsourcing model.

Any industry can apply this **PSPD** model in their business planning with the sole objective to spread its risks.

An activity you can do:

Every business needs to be thought in this direction. You may be an owner of a company, a salesperson or working at a senior level in an organization. Answer these:

1. How do you analyse profits? The way you make profits is one way. Another way is to look at where and how you can optimize costs, which is an indirect way to increase profits.
2. How can you scale your business?
3. Where are your markets?

4. Do you have the capabilities, the abilities, the bandwidth to handle more business?
5. Can you set an outsourcing model for your business before your hands are full and existing capacities are stressed?
6. How strong are you on forecasting your revenues, profits, the sales funnel? Do you have a mix of clients who give you business regularly, occasionally, once in a long-time?
7. Where do you prospect, do you have a long list of potential clients you are working on?
8. How well-spread are your business risks? I typically call them shock absorbers. If one vertical is not working to its potential, you have the others take the pressure to run the show. You need specialists to run each of these. It's up to you to decide if you need complementary business models which do not put pressure on your existing infrastructure and people or you want to get into radically different businesses. The point is to have various engines running.

9. Prepare to the fullest

To a great extent, this is a habit. Leaving no stone unturned is an attitude, and you can experience this from your childhood days. We often observe children, especially parents, when they say, “our child is very committed, he will not rest till he is not fully satisfied, he will not sleep, eat or even go to play till he completes his homework or some project undertaken. This attitude, for some reason, vanishes as we grow up, to a great extent because of multiple deadlines we face or simply because of the quantum of work and its complexity in today’s times.

But this act of preparing to the fullest is what came to the forefront for me when we were once working on a presentation we had to make.

As mentioned earlier, my relationship with the Tata Group grew every year, and I often visited their offices at the Bombay House in south Mumbai. Over the years, I had also learnt that the group meets once a year with all top senior management for their yearly plans in the presence of Mr. Ratan Tata. This thought gave me goosebumps, imagining the forum, the discussions, the product launches, strategic initiatives they would be discussing etc.

The Tata Group had become a key account for my company and everyone used to participate in its servicing. Every opportunity was like gold dust and there were multiple executives including me who had a role to play. Such was the canvas to handle this client that from my Directors who were more strategic and farming in nature to executives likes us who had become more hunters there, all were enjoying this process.

I remember we eventually got an opportunity to present ourselves at this strategic forum of the Tatas which was a dream come true. It was unbelievable and the day we got this confirmation it was a huge milestone for us. Everyone, from the top management was excited but there was Dushyant who had already started visualizing this presentation opportunity.

So, was this just another presentation? No, not all. There was a meeting called, where my learning of “preparing to the fullest” starts.

Remember, it was a time when Google was not loaded with content the way it is today, and we had to collect information on the Tata Group from all sources.

The research briefing was to find out everything on the Tata Group and the sources were:

- Annual Reports – last ten years
- Newsletters
- PR agencies
- Research Reports available in the public domain
- Stock market reports and Magazines
- All key product launches and their status today
- The senior management teams
- Their successes

- Their failures
- Their opportunities
- The strategic intents they must have mentioned in any forum.
- Their HR culture formed
- Their investor relationship initiatives
- Their vendor appointment models
- Their global plans
- Their interviews in the media – especially the senior management

Besides the above, the team was also told to get our data on:

- Last five year's sales with The Tata Group
- The people we regularly meet
- Our success stories
- Our failures, if any
- The scope for improvement etc. etc.

After a month's research, the team was ready with data of all kinds. I think we all knew Tata Group better than most of their employees working at the Bombay House at the end of that month.

The presentation's theme was ready, and the structure was put in place. The presentation was of a good number of slides, with the core message being how the Tata Group would need a strategic vendor like us in the coming years. It was all about their initiatives and how to fulfil their global ambitions; and how the print media through us would play an essential part in this journey.

I would want the reader to draw attention to how preparation can take you miles ahead in your tasks to be achieved. I will be honest in mentioning that probably more than seventy percent of the data collected was of no use for this presentation. We often used to wonder what we were doing, why so much effort, or how this would benefit but, in the end, it was all worth it. The data gave us enough confidence, and we could have handled any question or query which would have come in this meeting. We got a patient listening, and our presentation reflected our preparedness. Some questions were thrown at us, but they were not of data correction, but more of how we would drive the next steps and what help we would need as the team there listening to us, was convinced that we indeed are their strategic partner. Mission accomplished.

An activity you can do:

1. Prepare well for your meetings. I will insist, over-prepare.
2. Go through the last Minutes of your meetings, the unfinished agenda, the things you have not completed, pending from the client, the promises you made but not fulfilled and see how this meeting goes. You will be surprised how the meeting takes shape.
3. Focus on the research part before you meet new clients. Get insight on their business challenges, the pain areas they should be experiencing and what solutions you can offer.

10. Be ruthless to yourself, don't spare yourself first

Have you ever experienced instant success? I'm sure we all have in our lives at some point or the other. It's a pleasant surprise we get when we are least expecting results or something to happen, and there comes that surprise unexpectedly or before time. When this happens frequently, we call ourselves lucky, or we touch upon the threshold of over-confidence or a charm we possess that works consistently. Nothing wrong as long as it's working for us.

What happens when we keep working hard, but nothing happens? What happens when our repeated efforts and persistence don't fetch us anything? In Sales particularly, we put in those efforts to win a client, a deal or get that foot in the door, but it doesn't work for us beyond a point. I've seen many salespersons get grossly disappointed, and then they infect their colleagues, the negativity spreads faster, and the whole environment gets toxic. Watch out for such team members as these salespersons pull and suck out a lot of energy from the team, often leaving the others in a spot of bother. The leaders particularly get clueless, which can affect a lot of planning.

There was one sales executive on my team a few years back who was extremely good at his job. He was very meticulous in his planning, his approach was very punctual, but for some reason or the other didn't taste success as much as we all could have desired for him. With others performing well, a point came when he became a talk of the team, and others started empathizing with him, calling him unlucky.

Honestly, I was never worried about his non-performance. Somewhere, I knew he was right in his basics. I always believe in a process that takes time, but eventually, one succeeds what I always think. There's a good quote that says, "people call me lucky; I only work hard." This executive was working hard, but results were not coming in immediately, but I knew he was sowing seeds for the long-term.

Here's a story which inspired me:
The story of pushing the mountain –

A depressed man deprived of success asked God why is this happening to him despite all the efforts he was putting in. God listened and told him to push a mountain after waking up early in the morning for a few months. At first, the man was puzzled but listened to God and started pushing the mountain every day. After six months of seeing nothing happened, this man was upset and again called on to God and asked what difference this brought. The mountain stands in the same position, and he has not gained anything. God replied that he was told to push the mountain, not move it, which was not going to happen in any case. Coming to results, God said, the least this man's efforts yielded is that he's got a great body now, waking up early, he has cultivated a new habit, and overall looks in good shape.

The moral of the story is results sometimes are not seen immediately it takes time, but because of the efforts put in, the foundation is built, which we don't realize. One doesn't get what we always desire, but the steps make us reach somewhere and results come in from unexpected areas. This story is by Gaur Gopal Das.

Coming back to my executive, his efforts were also not wasted. After a few months, all the seeds he had sown started giving results. He got referred by his existing contacts made and won more deals than we all imagined. He went on to become one of my best executives. He got us a break in the Aditya Birla Group. We both visited Grasim, the flagship company of this Group and successfully closed a deal. After the Tata Group, an entry into the Aditya Birla Group was a significant milestone. It was the process which worked eventually. Had he not done his basics right, compromised on the steps, not followed-up with his clients, not built his relationship, it could have been a different story.

An activity you can do:

Do not stop there every time you face a hurdle or a block in getting through a deal. Ask yourself have you done everything needed to win that deal. Are you convinced you have left no stone unturned?

If the answer in your mind is a yes, move on to the next or else re-visit the whole process of winning the customer again.

11. Don't get exhausted; think exhaustively

This line I picked up from an experienced lawyer I was sitting with many years back. There was a case I had gone to discuss with him on, and he could see I was mentally tired on it. Several doors were shut on me, and I couldn't understand the way forward. This lawyer, a family friend, put his hand on my shoulder, offered me a cup of tea and said, "don't get exhausted; think exhaustively about how you can turn things around." This suggestion worked like magic on me, and sounded like how my father used to say, that there's a solution for every problem; you only need to assess the options and go ahead with your experience and instinct.

****

While working on a big client, Dushyant, my mentor, again mentioned something similar. He saw I was stuck on a few things, unable to decide from the options, and things were not moving as per our desire. He only said, "Think about all the options first. Write them on a piece of paper, absorb it thoroughly and then decide which is the best way forward in the given situation and go for it with all your energy". He further elaborated, think about ten ideas to make this happen. The very thought to list down ten ideas is a step in the right direction rather than looking at a black hole with no hope. The moment you think like this, options open up, not always ten ideas in number but some solutions start coming to you.

I've applied this process of thinking exhaustively, looking for solutions, and putting my best foot forward after assessing all options. I believe I have achieved subsequently, which otherwise looked impossible to me earlier. Is this an attitude? Maybe yes, but this works like magic as it helps me break all the shackles and believe in my actions. Well begun is half done as they say, and this approach only hurries the results sometimes going wrong but at least you progress rather than not doing anything.

The power of affirmation also works like magic. Think about how the scene would be post the problems getting solved, and you experience that later. One of the best books I've read on this subject is Power of the Subconscious Mind by Joseph Murphy.

An activity you can try:

1. Start meditation
2. Visualize the day or results you want to see going forward and stay in that zone when you close your eyes.
3. When facing challenges or problems, think about the possible solutions and work on the "what if" possibilities. What if you do this or do that, and what would be the outcome rather than not doing anything.

12. How many Doctors are there in Mumbai?

Post-September, we used to focus on the diaries and calendar business. With some great product samples, we had made, we were expected to take these around to our list of clients given, and it was all about hard-core selling. Being time-bound, we had to meet as many as we could, show samples, set the terms there and close the deal there itself. We were pretty equipped to close these deals. Still, due to customization, there was always scope to revert to the customer with their desired changes, terms, and features expected on these products.

A Pharmaceutical company was one client of mine with whom we had done business already, and it was expected for us to touch base with existing clients first before looking for new ones. I had a great meeting and happily rushed back to the office with a deal almost sure to win, but the client needed some additional quantity options, for which I had to check with the office. In the review meeting, I was asked what the extra quantity was but, most importantly, asked why they needed more. I had thought the "why" asked was very obvious from the client. I just felt they needed it and we should offer the new price. In the review meeting, the point made to me was to draw my attention that it was a pharma company. Whom will they give these diaries? I had an answer - to doctors with whom they were connected through their medical representatives and other sales channels. The point I missed to ask was if that was the case "how many doctors are there in Mumbai" and why they should order more and not the figure they had only asked me to quote? I had missed the big picture, in short, an opportunity.

Often in our glory moment, salespersons forget to assess the bigger picture. We are satisfied and happy that the order has swelled but don't make an effort to explore how further it can go up if we ask the right questions. In this case, if I had thrown in questions like:

- Why do you need these additional quantities?

- How do you intend to distribute them to all?
- Besides your connected doctors, how can we help you reach more doctors to whom these can be sent?

Just by triggering the right questions, the customer feels we are not just selling but wanting to help them grow their business, and as vendors of a different kind, we are ready to help them achieve their objectives. The difference between a good vendor to great vendor lies here.

Do not lose an opportunity when your customer reacts to your offer beyond the asked specifications, terms and standards. The customer is always thinking beyond what you have imagined, and it is here you need to ask them questions. Every right question can open up new opportunities and an opportunity for you to impress and open up a new dialogue.

This incident got my mind going, and I could sense an explosion in my mind. The key point for readers to note is how to measure the potential of your clients?

An activity you can do:

1. Do you know the potential of your customer's business?
2. Do you know how much your customer should buy from you not how much he has bought or always will buy. Help your customer take the right decisions.
3. List down the names of your existing clients and think about how many buy all your products or services you sell, the ones who buy a few, and there will be names of a few more who only buy a very small quantity. This strategy itself is the potential list, to begin with. Upselling starts here.
4. Make a list of clients you can reach but have never thought about earlier. It's all about creating blue oceans for your business. While the competition works in red oceans, create blue oceans where there's enough space and scope. I've mentioned a book you can read on this subject of blue oceans at the end of the book.

13. Where there is a mess, there is an opportunity

Usually, you give a great platform to perform, and even a mediocre person will provide results. When you have a great product, a great value-added feature with little or no competition, do you think you need a great salesperson with extraordinary skills and talent to get results? Probably not.

The scene changes when you are one amongst the many out there. With no differentiators in your product or service offer and a red ocean in which you operate, your selling, relationship building and execution skills matter and is tested ruthlessly.

We were operating from an industrial estate mentioned earlier. It's a place where the best of brains can get demoralized. Compared to an independent factory these are not best of the places to work. Nevertheless, we, as salespersons, were leading from the front. Getting business was tough but getting it executed was a nightmare. With an almost significant portion of operations outsourced, adhering to deadlines, monitoring the work in progress was more stressful than winning a deal. We were expected to keep track of all this and ensure the final product was delivered as planned. Sometimes it used to baffle me as to why we are responsible for someone else's tasks but honestly, no one had an answer.

On one such evening, when I was pretty burdened because of the operational execution responsibilities, my managing director Romi Vohra called me who could sense my turmoil. He told me which helped me pass through that phase and look at the days ahead as something to learn from. He told me that in areas of mess and chaos lie opportunities to understand and lead that no book can teach you. I realized eventually that while I was in the print industry selling print products, I was not technically educated in the sense of having passed a diploma or holding a degree from a printing college. We were primarily in sales, and as a strategy, the company hired people who were not related to this industry nor studied printing. We were groomed as salespersons, and everything to do with winning in sales was taught to us. Here was an opportunity of learning most brutally; because of the unorganized nature of the industry and our infrastructure, which was not in place, we were getting a hands-on opportunity to learn from ground zero.

In our journey from order confirmation to execution right up to the collection of money, we were exposed to all stages. Over time we could gauge the different papers by touch and feel, all the technical aspects of the calculation of paper volume, the printing process, the time to be taken in production, the estimation of costs, and even working on a date plan from order confirmation to delivery we could assess with ease. Before I could realize I was entirely unknowingly part of the print industry.

Whenever you are made to work into situations you do not belong, the easiest thing to do is to quit or get frustrated, but take a pause and think what best you can do in the given situation. If the misery gets on you to an extent you cannot tolerate, you can quit, but if not, if you see any scope of learning, stick to it and figure out how it can help you eventually. Time changes, people change, circumstances change faster and suddenly before you realize you are back on track. It has happened to me many times. I learnt from my experience that nothing goes to waste. The time I spent on the floors of the industrial estates, all that made me strong and educated me to handle clients of all kinds. My learnings enabled me to enter even international markets where the print industry is much more organized, and the customers are more informed. Needless to mention but I was more comfortable there as I was groomed at a level where there were many challenges.

14. The handshake which brought ten lacs

In general, we all know the importance of good body language. It is a part of the over communication skill we need to possess, particularly if you happen to be in sales, marketing or any front-end or back-end activities concerning customers you are in touch with. Back-end also because voice, vocabulary and pronunciation become your most potent skill sets.

Despite all that we know, here are some inputs and tips (a few taken from Subroto Bagchi's book "Sell") for presentations that every salesperson has to make to their customers.

- Prepare your presentation thoroughly. A day before, make sure you know the content flow and are prepared for any questions which may come up.

- Not only for such presentations but asking the audience how much time you have together gives the proper signal to all. It also helps you to pace the content appropriately. Many people spend a lot of time on something which doesn't need the extended time and rush at the end when the core of the content is to be discussed.

- Begin with your customer in mind, not you or your business. This presence of mind is likely to get the utmost and quick attention.

- Try setting a context and personalize it. A story form works brilliantly to set the tone. For example, if it is for selling insurance most of the time, I've seen people talking about the schemes, benefits, premiums, etc., but start with a story to tell how your recommendation worked with someone you know who stood to benefit. If the context is similar to your prospect's age and earnings, he will relate to it more closely.

- Make the slides more process-driven to keep the listeners hooked on to your offer. Navigating your listener's thoughts to what you want them to think works in your favour, or else the audience will lose interest and will not be in sync with your story and offer, which you have to come to eventually. Keeping the audience hooked is an art and customize it every time.

A school of thought also says sending the presentation in advance can help you set the tone, but I'm not too fond of this as this defeats the very purpose. With minimum content, more bullet points (I also hate to use the word bullets - as it kills) or highlights, don't think of how you expect the audience to understand only by reading it. If reading helps, why present now or later.

- Have a conversation and do not say, "we will reserve the questions at the end" why? I like to say stop me when you have a question because that means my audience is listening to me and engaging with me.

- Body language and eye contact - get this spot on, or else a rich in content can also go down the drain.

- It is fundamental as it may sound but do not start with "I hope I am audible or can the last person hear me". I've seen the audience hates to hear this.

Also, arrive at the venue in advance check the audio, video, slides on the laptop, chargers, back-ups, everything is in place, and prepare for the worst-case scenario. What happens if there is a power failure and there's a blackout. I've carried candles in my bag with a matchbox and a white chart paper with glue tapes and pens in case there isn't a whiteboard in the room. If I can talk about the context and my story, I don't need the slides as my offer can always follow later.

- Few more basics - spell checks, correct current logo of your customer's company, names of people to thank (spelling and pronunciations) - all this have to be accurate with absolutely no scope for errors.

- Carrying a hard copy of the presentation is a good back up again to carry in case there's a request for you to leave something behind.

- Most importantly, I've learnt that noting action points is hugely critical. Make sure you appoint someone from your team to take notes, and trust me, make this person write everything - I mean everything. Besides the key action points which emerged from the presentation, the follow-up, who walked in first, last, their body language, the ones who changed expressions at which slide, who asked which question, the eye communication of the audience wanting to talk to eachother, the affirmations you received at which slide etc. etc. All this when you revisit later helps immensely to strategize further.

- You can also record the audio or the video of the entire presentation but seek their approval or permission before you switch on these gadgets.

Another essential skill a salesperson has to possess is body language. Wikipedia defines body language as "Body language is a type of communication in which physical behaviours, as opposed to words, are used to express or convey the information. Such behaviour includes facial expressions, body posture, gestures, eye movement, touch and the use of space". I've always emphasized the importance of good body language to my team members. Have a firm handshake with men but don't crush a lady's hand with your hand grip.

Here's one story on how a good handshake can impact your prospect:

We were at the Shipping Corporation of India in south Mumbai and I had visited the client with a colleague of mine who was trying to pitch there. My colleague led the talk, and I played a supportive role there. As usual, at the end of the meeting, we shook hands with the customer and said goodbye. It was a good meeting, but we knew we would have to come here repeatedly and win this customer with our persistence. Just as we were about to take the elevator downstairs, an office assistant from the customer's office called out to us and said the customer wanted to see us again. We both went into his cabin again. At first, we thought we must have forgotten something there, or he wanted to give us a sample of his previous work to look at, but it was for something else. Another gentleman in his cabin appeared to be his colleague was also present, and our customer pointed his finger at me. I was confused and got a bit worried about what must have happened, but I was in for a delightful surprise. The customer smiled at me and said Rajnish; I've not shaken hands with anyone as you did today; it was so firm and professional, and I liked your tight grip, which gave me so much confidence. He further said he couldn't stop telling his colleague, who was equally impressed and wanted to meet me and experience the handshake again. Wow! Would you believe this. Here's a case - not my direct customer as I was just helping my colleague, I spoke the least, was at ease as my colleague was leading the meeting, but all I did, as usual at the end, was shaked hands which impressed the customer. After all these years, the handshake was something I remember, and my colleague then told me that in his subsequent visits to that customer, I was often remembered and referred to as the handshake man.

This incident also broke the ice with the customer. In sales, customizing and adapting to situations as per what customers want to talk and hear is what works well in your conversations and engagement. I've discussed the weather in the UK most with my customers there (which is what they like), the traffic in Mumbai, politics, football, technology, new book launched and the game of cricket is another favourite topic people want to discuss. Find out what works with your customer and stick to that. In this case, it was the handshake.

An activity you can do:

1. Ideally, you can do it for all your clients but start with the top ten or fifteen.
2. List down the names of your customers, basically the decision-makers.
3. List down their likes and dislikes, hobbies, habits etc. If you don't know these, start the process of knowing from today onwards and start revolving your conversations around these the next time you interact with them and see how your engagement graph goes up.

15. Believe in your instinct

What your heart says is often correct vis-à-vis the mind in situations of uncertainty. I know it's tough, but this is my experience. I've often seen myself in cases where you need to take that decision, and I have chosen to go with what the inner voice tells me. In his book, Narayan Murthy, Chairman of Infosys, writes, "In God, we trust, for everything else we need data." Though inspirational, this sentence can be put to the test if you cannot decide even after having the data and all the inputs. What do you do?

****

Here are a few of my stories:

This was at a time when I had just graduated and had started my professional journey. After spending a week at a Chartered Accountant's office to do the Articleship, I felt uncomfortable being a part of it. I couldn't see myself becoming a CA spending most of my time at a desk. I had just graduated, and on a piece of advice from a close relative who was a well-wisher, I had taken admission to become a CA, but I was quite a misfit there. This realization and the step ahead were the most challenging decisions I had to make, an apparent conflict of mind and my heart. Finally, I listened to my heart and dropped the idea to become a CA.

****

Another turning point came when I got a job opportunity with ICICI Prudential Life Insurance in the second year of my professional life. I got selected and could have become their Distributor, but I didn't accept the offer. While I like the Banking, Financial Services & Insurance industry for the potential it holds, I thought in the early part of my career I wanted to work for a small company. A place to work where things are to be built, where opportunities are in plenty to perform, and one gets to take initiatives in areas other than your core responsibility.

****

Then there was a company called Essel Packaging, who had offered me the post of a Management Trainee with a three-year posting in Egypt which I didn't take up. While this was exciting as it would have got me into international exposure very early in my life, I didn't feel it was the right time to stay away from my mother. I had lost my father three years before this offer came in, and we were just about settling down and coming to terms. Had I taken up, my mother would have felt the void.

****

After a successful three-year period with Print House India, where I used to work, I was called by my Directors one day. I was leading a team of eight Business Heads, and each had about five people, a mix of sales, customer service and production coordinators under them. Collectively I was responsible for their business and leading them for a fifty-crore business revenue. This phase was one of the highlights of my career.

The Directors called me for a discussion on the way forward. With different sales verticals performing well, businesses having enough traction and a direction to work upon, I was told to look at international markets - to enter exports. This incident was by far one of the most significant turning points of my career. I was honest in telling them that my knowledge of exports was from the books I've read in my graduation days and the exposure doing my business management courses. I told them I've only read in books on a Letter of Credit, Bill of Lading and a Packing credit. Jokingly, the Directors also said the same thing - they also have no exposure but were ready to back me up rather than just throwing me in the waters.

I accepted the offer, and my journey in exports started. I learnt the hard way - visiting clients participating in fairs & exhibitions all across Africa, the UK, the US, Europe and the UAE. I failed on many fronts, learnt the trade tricks, understood the terms, processes, and steps the world followed, set my standard operating procedures, and then tasted success.

When I started my print management vertical, this experience came into the picture and helped us replicate the success with a new set of clients besides a few old ones who were happy to work with me.

In our endeavour to grow our export business, a few of the decisions we took were never attempted by our industry, which worked to our great advantage. Our regular practice, consistency, and, most importantly, our belief that we will find our footage proved right only because we trusted our instinct.

****

One of our other verticals, which focuses on exports & international market development consulting, is also a result of a gut feeling. I could sense there is a tremendous scope for the small businesses to grow, there's a hunger amongst them to take their business to the next level, to enter exports, but they fear, they are uncertain, they do not know the steps. We entered this space with our enrolment to various networking forums, connected to small businesses (MSMEs) and set the ball rolling. Besides running our own export business, we also coach and consult small companies to enter exports.

16. Little gems of wisdom – absorb how much you can

I'm blessed to be a reader, and I love books. Little did I realize but the sight of a good book, a recommended one, some which I hear about from someone, few which you see the covers of at bookstores and get excited, these things grew in my mind over a while. Eventually, it convinced me that a companion I always wanted, a friend who can tell me good things, alert me on the wrong steps, give me deep insight is what I will get from books. But a well-read person is not as important as how well that person has absorbed knowledge from the books they read. Execution and implementation matter the most.

Those little gems that I highlight reading a good book, the smile I get on my face when I read something very appealing, the deep meaning I'm able to derive from something very sparkling I've learnt is what matters the most to me. I recently got a wooden cabinet for myself for my books, and it was a dream sight to see a few of my books neatly displayed there. Finally, the books were breathing out from the closed shelf I had them in earlier. One evening, I randomly picked up a book from there and flipped through a few pages, going through my notes and highlighted portions. The book looked new to me again. The ideas were refreshed, and it was a new perspective I was reading again from.

In the following pages, you will find critical aspects from the books I read which appealed to me. While the books themselves are masterpieces and I will try and elaborate on the highlights, most importantly, I will try and connect with what and how it can be related to us as readers.

Here are a few of my all-time favourite books and my key takeaways.

Title: Odyssey: Pepsi to Apple by John A Byrne

The core idea behind this Book:

An autobiography by John Sculley, former Apple CEO, and John A. Byrne in August 1987, published by Harper & Row. In Odyssey, Sculley describes his time as CEO of PepsiCo and Apple during the late 1970s and early 80s. In discussing his transition from Pepsi's president and CEO to marketing visionary of Apple Computers, the author shares his insights into marketing and management strategies and forecasts future business trends.

Key takeaways and What's in for us:

- Primarily this book is very close to my heart because, if my memory serves me right, this was the first book I read correctly after my formal education. This book was spotted by me in my Director's cabin when I started my career in 1992, and I was curious to know what this is about due to the catchy title name.

- This book talks about Apple's strategy.

- The most exciting part of the book is about, you guessed it, Steve Jobs. Sculley seems to take pride in removing Jobs from an operational role within the company while maintaining him as a figurehead. Shortly after, Jobs left Apple to start NeXT, taking some of Apple's best people with him, while Sculley was CEO. Sculley defeated Jobs in a high stakes corporate drama and managed to turn around the company by making Apple more "business-friendly."

- We know how things turned out after NeXT. Jobs returned to Apple to make history. Apple bought NeXT and Jobs got his way back to the top. What I found interesting is the degree of attachment Jobs has to Apple – namely, how much he cared. Sculley frequently refers to how emotional he got, especially when Sculley removed him from operations with the Board's approval. The passion and thinking are well captured in this book.

- A great perspective on running an organization and dealing with challenging personalities. This book is timeless lesson leaders need to understand.

Finally, that one sentence from the book which shook me entirely is, *"Do you want to sell sugar water for the rest of your life, or do you want to come with me and change the world?"* What Steve Jobs said to Pepsi executive John Sculley to lure him to Apple. This sentence is one hard pitch made by none other than Steve himself - a masterstroke in talent acquisition. Sculley said the question landed like "a punch to the gut."

When Sculley took Steve Jobs up on his offer, Jobs did not have many close friends. "He was too busy putting a dent in the universe," says Sculley. Sculley became like an older brother to Jobs eventually.

Title: Zero to One by Peter Theil

The core idea behind this Book:

Zero to One is about how to build companies that create new things.

Key Takeaways and What's in for us:

- *"The next **Bill Gates** will not build an operating system. The next **Larry Page** of Google will not make another Search engine, or the next **Mark Zuckerberg** will not make another social network site."*

- This makes me think about innovation. How crucial are innovation and that bright idea required for that exponential success? Having a me-too product or service or a business model tested earlier can also get you going if you know the little things that are unmet yet but to make that significant impact; a new idea will get you that attention, funding, customers and success consistently.

- *"Characteristics of Monopoly - Proprietary technology, Network effects, Economies of Scale and Branding"*

- The Oxford Dictionary defines Monopoly as "the complete control of trade in particular goods or the supply of a particular service."

But nowhere above in the characteristics mentioned by the Author does he say control, product or service.

If you have technology that benefits you to run your business more efficiently than others in your industry, your network amongst industry players, vendors, resources and customers, if you have large-scale operations and never compromise on marketing and branding, you will have a leadership situation eventually. From Google Facebook to local players in your industry, think why they are so successful in getting that answer from this definition of Monopoly.

- *"If you choose the wrong partners or hire the wrong people – it may sometimes take a crisis of bankruptcy to repair or correct it. As a founder – your first job is to get the first thing right – you cannot build a great company on a flawed foundation."*

- Priceless lesson in Human Resources.

- The above statement helps me connect with Jim Collins's book – Good to Great. He says Get the right people in the right seat of your bus. Get the wrong people off the bus and then decide the way to your destination.

- *"Talented people don't need to work for you; they have plenty of options. You will attract employees if you explain your mission and why you are doing something important which no one else is doing."*

- Here's the best way to describe why purpose is more important. Knowing where you intend to go is inspirational to the people who will join you; the tasks ahead become relatively easy despite all the challenges.

- There were times when people worked for money, not that they don't do today but as the world generally progressed and the gap between rich and poor, underprivileged and the blessed ones reduced, employees look for something else in today's world. Aspirations matter and should be for the good progress one wants to make, but the passion for work, the purpose you are hooked on, the culture you create that stays with employees forever.

- As they say, people don't quit companies; they quit the people they work with. If you can give them the direction and purpose inspiring enough, they will be a part of your organization for a long time.

- *"Superior Sales and Distribution by itself can create a monopoly, even with no product differentiation."*

- As mentioned earlier, unless you have a path-breaking out of the box idea, you are another player in the crowded tested market out there.

- So, what happens to the businesses who are offering me-too products and services. Let's accept you cannot keep innovating for its sake, but yes, you can differentiate.

- Better, improved, enhanced, more engaging, easy to use etc., these words attract.

- How can we improve sales, customer service, and distribution experience better than the number one player in our industry does?

- Can we list down "how can our customer experience rage or be dissatisfied about?" rather than "how can we better customer experience." Focusing on what not to do can sometimes be easier than the other way around.

- *"It's much better to be the last mover - that is, to make the final significant development in a specific market and enjoy years or even decades of monopoly profits. The way to do that is to dominate a small niche and scale up from there toward your ambitious long-term vision."*

- We've heard about first-mover advantage but the last mover? This last mover strategy was exciting when I think it over.

- In time-tested markets, products and services which are always attractive, there's a general tendency to think there isn't space to step in for the competition. Sometimes created and often a result of being not well informed, we believe we cannot make money in these segments, nor is there a scope for getting any market share.

- It will be interesting to again get an insight into these segments, markets etc. and find out where there are gaps or the unmet scope which still exists.

- We've seen what happened to Nokia, Kodak's digital cameras, the Blackberrys, and many more where entering their strong, established markets was considered absurd once. Still, innovative companies did, and today they have been wiped out to a great extent.

- Think even in terms of small businesses and local competition where there can be opportunities you can launch as a last mover. A brilliant strategy to consider.

- *"The best thing I did as a Manager at PayPal was to make every person in the Company responsible for doing just one thing. Every employee's one thing was unique, and everyone knew I would evaluate him on that one thing. Simplify the task of managing people. Most fights inside a company happen when colleagues compete for the same responsibilities."*

- Let us not confuse here with job responsibilities or profiles which may have many things to do. Multi-tasking is a must for today's employees.

- But I like what he writes here – just one unique thing for which an employee is hired on what he will be majorly assessed at the end of the year. It simplifies everything to know if a person is an asset, contributing or just a passenger who is also needed for different objectives.

- *"Like acting, sales works best when hidden. See the job titles - people who sell advertising are called "Account Executives." People who sell customers work in "Business Development." people who sell companies are called*

"Investment Bankers," and people who sell themselves are called "Politicians." There's a reason for these redescriptions: none of us wants to be reminded when we're being sold."

- This is a brilliant explanation of why people don't like to be sold.
- Imagine for a while regarding the above examples if the titles were had "Sales" slipped in somehow; how would we think when they talked to us?
- The key message is "sales work best when hidden."
- Don't sell when you are selling. Explain what's in for your customer, the value, the offer and he will find it attractive.

Title: The High-Performance Entrepreneur by Subroto Bagchi

A special note:

This is a book that I will strongly recommend to anyone wishing to get into entrepreneurship. You would find many books on this topic, but here's one from a very practical side. This book deeply impacted me when I started my venture in 2012. I've implemented many of the gems mentioned herein and find great value in them. I glance through this book very often to get the sparks once again.

Key Takeaways and What's in for us:

- *"This book is not about how to start a company. It is about creating high-performance entrepreneurs."*

- Here's the critical aspect. Read the above sentence again. It's not about the different things we need to be ready for to start a new company. The keywords here are "creating high-performance entrepreneurs." It would help if you had a different mindset to create something high-performing in nature from the start. The Author explains the traits you need to have which go a long way in your professional life.

- *"If the leaders do not demonstrate frugality, building the requisite culture in an upcoming organization is tough. That must be borne out by demonstrated behaviour right at the top."*
- *"Comfort with postponed gratification is a critical requirement of entrepreneurship."*

- Let us accept this. When we read about top leaders - may it be political or corporate or even actors, the kind of salaries, money they make, what comes to our mind? These guys mint money; they earn extraordinarily, right? Don't get me wrong; I'm not saying making colossal money is bad - in fact, you have to make money in business. The point is, leading a life with frugality goes a long way to building a culture of content and satisfaction. We all know there's no end to what you can buy and enjoy once you start making that money much more than what you need or want, but if you learn to hold back and be happy in what you need, you will get that inner peace.

- *"If even remotely, the thought of safety net haunts you and you cannot talk yourself out of it, you are not ready to sail. When you build an organization, your comforts must be subordinate to all other interests. Finally, there cannot be thoughts of exit options in the event of a failure."*

- Entrepreneurship is one way: no looking back, no exit options. Honestly, in the first six months, it did come across to my mind to go back to employment, but when I read this sentence, it did give me courage.

- Freedom to experiment, de-risk and spread across multiple revenue streams is what I thought about, and we could sail through.

- The ability to make quick decisions, dare to think differently and believe in what I'm doing helped when I came out of my safety net.

- *"We are three good friends, and we have this fantastic idea. We want to start a company. Tell us how?"*

- Every reader who wished to start a company would relate to this. In our excitement, in our belief of a non-researched idea or thought, we often fall prey to this.

- *"While having a fantastic idea is a great starting point unless there is a reasonable view of what larger business the company can be in, the life of an enterprise can be very short-lived."*

- Here again, the keyword is to know the bigger picture. The ability to measure potential, market depth and width, the SWOT of the idea, which is so crucial -

unless one doesn't get to the root of your fantastic idea, you cannot take that long-term.

- *"My career is not getting anywhere. I hate this company, and I do not like my boss. I want to start a company".*

- Unlike the earlier generation, this mindset has grown in recent times. Call it the entrepreneurial spirit, the success of start-ups with the funding they get, the opportunities, the ease of forming a venture, the tech-based approach, whatever. Still, if you ever start a company because you are unhappy at work, it's the first step for disaster.

- *"If you do not need the money, do not start a company."*

- Making money is essential when you are running your venture. If you don't like to earn money and want to "give back to society" or "serve the country," the author says that there are many other ways by which you can do that. I like when he says, "if you do not love money, it is unlikely that you will ever understand the nuances of generating wealth." It is unlikely he thinks you will ever know the difference between a paying customer and an admirer of your work.

Profile of an Entrepreneur: The author then mentions these crucial traits:

- **"Self-confidence."**

He says the most critical ingredient, and I couldn't agree more. If you cannot believe in your ideas, products, services, no one else will. Even a little shake-up in these, and you are probably finished if you think of an exit. You may face challenges, hurdles and near impossible situations, but the ability to rise can only happen if you are super-confident.

- **"To determine your entrepreneurial streak, ask yourself the below:"**

1. Did you take vital decisions in your life, or did someone else invariably take them for you?
2. Did you enjoy the process, irrespective of the outcome?
3. How did you handle small adversities?
4. Did you ever feel helpless?
5. Did you decide, or did you allow situations to determine the courses?

6. Can you make friends with strangers?
7. Do you know your physical and mental limitations? Do you think you can overcome them?
8. Do you feel comfortable talking about yourself?
9. Do you feel comfortable asking others for help?
10. Does the act of buying and selling excite you?
11. Do you like meeting people?
12. Do you see things to completion?

I've heard a lot of people who have been successful entrepreneurs. We do this for inspiration, but if one tries to answer these questions, you will know if you can go the entrepreneurial way.

- *"Supply-Chain, ERP, Data-warehousing etc. etc. - none of these words existed in the original business plan we had written. Entrepreneurship requires the ability to read patterns on the wall, flexibility and an uncanny ability to seize the moment".*

- After reading the above, I couldn't sleep for a few days. The humble and modest business plan I had prepared was looking more of a wish list to me. This sentence taught me not to look too far ahead but just establish the core and get nimble in our business model. This thought of skill and strategic flexibility changed our business forever.

- We wanted to start in Print Management (PM) (offering print services to clients through outsourcing – not having our infrastructure but outsource to strategic vendors carefully selected) and Print Consulting (PC) – utilizing my experience in print and grooming aspiring printers to develop their business, help them enter exports.

- In December 2021, we will complete eight years in business. Today we continue to offer the print management services as that's our core but have stopped print consulting as the model didn't work long-term. Printers expected sales to be done by us on their behalf and wanted shortcuts to success. Many couldn't understand that developing business and entering international markets is a marathon, not a sprint. Out of the many we used to consult, two remained with us who understood the game well taught by us and today are our primary strategic partners.

We added other verticals to our business over a while –

- Recruitment services, which is led by my business partner with her team.

- Consulting on Strategic Marketing & Exports was born out of my passion for these functions. I deliberately formed this to remain in touch with the small and medium enterprises that need these services. There's a great hunger and aspiration to grow their business, and they need professionals to guide and take them through. With our core business established, we network not to develop this consulting business aggressively but to build relationships primarily. A big lesson learnt was developing and building a network when you do not need new business.

- We also tried e-Commerce briefly but quit when we realized it's a different ball game and not our core.

- We resisted the temptation to enter manufacturing – to set up a printing unit.

- All these experiments I could do because of the entrepreneurship platform I had for myself. It was fine to fail when things were obscure, but finally, we found the right direction.

- The learning and experiments will not stop as we will be hungry to see the patterns on the wall.

- *"When you build a team, you do not start by looking at compatibility and sameness. You look for complementary skills and diversity. In a founding company, the core team must possess from day one - the ability to bring business, produce and deliver, read numbers and negotiate with investors. These qualities must be innate in the starting team".*

- This ultimately solved my problem of who would be my partners in crime. It was not my best friend or a relative I was close to, but it was with someone I trusted first and foremost and someone who had complementary skills.

- With Swapnali Haryan, my business partner, we run our business successfully because the skills are complementary. I love to work on areas I have my strengths in, and there are others that she gets value tremendously and leads on her own. Sometimes, we may have creative differences, but we are on the same page nine out of ten times.

- Extending further on the above, we also looked at outsourcing our non-core work – legal, banking, accounts, social media and website creation. These vendors and consultants have been on our panel for several years with excellent compatibility ensuring we work hassle-free and focus on what we are good at. As this author also says, "every individual must be closely associated with the business-creation process, either you bring business, or you execute. Everyone else is an overhead". We practice exactly this.

- *"Take resilience out, and you just cannot become an entrepreneur. It is not the greatness of an idea or an individual, but the sheer ability to hang on that helps create great organizations. If you can hold on to the reef for the night, tomorrow is another day".*

- This happened to us too. It is not a rosy day every day. Things go wrong, plans fail, customers are lost overnight for reasons least expected, markets change, policies change, and all these can significantly affect your mindset.

- Entrepreneurship is a one-way ticket, and there's no looking back. The temptation to quit does come up when things go wrong, especially in the initial years. Personal events can also make you think twice. One such personal event was when my partner was expecting her second child after three months of our start. I could see she had come to the office that day with a clear mindset to tell me she needed to quit, and she asked me this question: "how can we wind up as she will not be in a position going forward to work or contribute in any manner." At the end of our hour-long discussion, she was convinced we could continue, she could still work from home and was relieved we could find a solution.

- Then it was a day when we lost one of our biggest consulting clients as they had run out of money to fund to promote a revolutionary product they had created. This incident shook us up as the majority of our cash flow was from this client, but we could sustain it because of a carefully planned forecasting model we had in place. Most importantly, the de-risking strategy helped us sail through.

- *"The six-horse chariot strategy. Six equally strong horses would pull the business in the same direction, at the same time with the same energy.*

The six horses are:

- *Domain* – the core, which is our print management

- *Tools* – The tools to acquire customers, manage them, service them and sow seeds for future growth.

- *Methodology* – we've found what works and what doesn't over a period and keep improving to simplify things with customers at the core.

- *Quality* – we are incredibly passionate about how we treat and respond to customers, the little things, and all customer touchpoints, the quality of work is all over. We've set very high standards with SOPs in place and a clear to-do list for the vendors and us regarding the print products we produce. We were fortunate we worked primarily for the developed markets, which invariably bring high quality, procurement and execution standards in a way that helped. The crucial thing is that we also got all those practices to our domestic business line for consulting and print management.

- *Innovation* - it need not be an innovation of products only. Innovation is a mindset, and we introduced certain firsts in our consulting models like on-board association, hand-holding rather than only preaching, fee relating to success etc.

- *Branding* - while B2B businesses don't focus much on this, it's the ability to be visible in the correct forums which we concentrate on. From the day we created our logo, our logo colours to the website and social media presence are all in sync, with a high recall value.

- *"The thirty golden rules for getting the early customers":*

The ones which caught my attention and something I worked on are:

- *Write to all your contacts from the past without exception and any expectations."*

- I did this. I gathered all my courage as I started my entrepreneurial journey and received a great response almost from everyone. Few of those converted, and those clients have been with me ever since. The rest who did not convert to sales are also in touch and are advocates of my sincerity, commitment, and appreciation of our work. They are also on my social media connections which gets me further benefits.

- *"Go back to people who disqualified you in a bidding round."*

-This strategy again is a part of your persistence. I've observed clients appreciate we didn't take losing a deal as the end of the world. Most importantly, the clients know whom to fall upon if they need our services for more work or just in case the selected vendor fails in deliverables.

- *"Visit trade shows."*

- Attending industry-specific trade shows and fairs is a part of our overall marketing strategy. We plan our budgets to spend where it is required the most with no compromise. I attend The Frankfurt Book Fair, The London Book Fair and the Bologna Book Fair consistently. It's a platform to meet your existing clients; we discuss the weather, curse the traffic etc. everything, and the meetings end with something to act upon for the next six months. The fairs allow me to showcase my work and then take it from there with new clients. We've won several clients only because we were there. The good part is the pre-visit marketing we do. We write emails, connect them on social media and drop in a line to say we are attending the respective fair, and then it's easy to get an appointment.

- *"Become a member of the right industry bodies. Seek opportunities for participation and speaking engagements".*

-This networking strategy proved to be a master strategy. I grabbed every opportunity to get visibility from the various networking platforms I became a member of. I've observed nothing works better than meeting someone in person and expressing with all your speaking and body language strengths, which helps make that impact.

- *"Have a great website in place."*

This is one thing we do very seriously. Our marketing budget's most significant share is website making, maintenance and social media marketing. The website has to be perfect on all fronts - technically, up to date on what you offer, loaded with good content and value, engaging and something which makes the visitor take action to contact you.

- *"Do not fall into the Tender Loving Call (TLC) trap of repeatedly pitching to a sympathetic person who cannot give you business but is always very nice to you. Save your energy and without fear of rejection, make real sales calls on wooden-faced tough-talking prospects".*

-I loved this to the core, as we all do this in our lives no matter what. It has to do a lot with the art of prospecting also. Know your customer, the rejections, the funnel process, and you will realize there's no point wasting your time on something which isn't working at all as the world doesn't end there. It also tells me about the red and blue ocean strategy. Read this brilliant book: The Blue Ocean Strategy by Renée Mauborgne and W. Chan Kim.

- *"Speak to the person sitting next to you - in an airplane, a business lounge, a dentist's waiting area or an industry event and ask him what he does."*

-First and foremost, it helps you overcome your fear of talking to strangers. The keyword in the above sentence is "ask him what he does." Most of the time, people want to pitch, tell on what they do and rush on everything–asking what the stranger does helps break the ice easily as everyone likes to talk about themselves. Be a good listener, and somewhere in the conversation, you will notice the pain areas. Once you get a feel of it, you may address the pain areas yourself if he is your potential customer, or you can recommend him to someone you know who can help. Trust me, either way, you have a new relationship that will help you in the future.

- *"You must love money. Respect money—transparency and maintaining a record of all transactions help. Always overestimate costs and underestimate your revenues. If you do not have an order pipeline healthy enough for the first two quarters in a service business, it is unlikely that you will meet your annual numbers. Four crucial ratios to look at Gross margins, Earnings Before Interest, Tax, Depreciation and Amortization (EBITDA), Profit before Tax as a percentage of Sales (PBT) and the ratio of billable versus non-billable people."*

- When I started my venture, my good friend Suresh Ramakrishnan also advised me on cashflow. He said to watch your cashflow always. From the day we began to date, we maintain six sheets that capture all we need to know about our business in one glance every month. These six sheets capture our sales - pipeline and in-hand, collections, cashflow, receivables, clients in the development stage and expense records. We work on a yearly budget but review it every quarter for course correction.

- *"When you build your own business, make sure you deal with the customer directly as much as possible."*

-My takeaway from this is that though one may eventually develop a team in sales and acquire new customers if I'm the owner of a business, I need to know my customer well. As companies grow, the top guys do not get time to spend with their best customers. Scheduling time to meet your top twenty should not be a challenge at least once a year.

Title: Good to Great by Jim Collins

The core idea behind this Book:

Why Some Companies Make the Leap... and Others Don't is a management book by Jim C. Collins that describes how companies transition from good to great and where they fail to make the transition.

Key takeaways and What's in for us:

- *"The good-to-great companies did not focus principally on what to do to become great; they focused equally on what not to do and what to stop doing."*

- An absolute masterclass of a statement from Jim Collins. The above summarizes and answers most of the questions that any start-up, newly established company, or even an established one is looking for in terms of how to grow, go to the next level, etc.

- *"First who....then what: We found instead that they (good-to-great leaders on strategy) they first got the right people on the bus, the wrong people off the bus, and the right people in the right seats".*

- When I read this sentence, it gives me goosebumps. The entire people and growth strategy can be captured in this one sentence.

- I will go further in applying this to even external contact points of yours - vendors, bankers, consultants etc. - Once you select the right people in the right seat for the right job, everything falls in place. How often do we say leave it to them, and it will do done? I'm confident or if that's the vendor, rest assured the work will be done on time. We say that because we know we have the right people on the job at the right place.

- Basically, we need people who match our wavelengths, have the right capabilities, and they will deliver. Selecting people on board, your employees, vendors anyone to provide work for your company can be easy once you have this strategy in place.
- We've done this in our way – changed our outsourced Accounts agency three times, till we finally met a young Chartered Accountant who thinks and sets standards of services just like how we do for our customers. Then our Bankers, fortunately, selected a private Bank that suits us on technology, options, services, etc. We've hardly visited them in years. Few of our key vendors are also with us ever since we started our business, which proves this point.

- *"The moment you feel the need to manage someone tightly, you've made a hiring mistake."*

- This is a great HR strategy we've adapted also. A person comes on board, and I observe besides skills and knowledge which I could judge from the interview and what's written on that person's CV is the attitude. The ASK principle I've followed stands for – A for Attitude, S for Skill and K for Knowledge. Now the problem is skills and knowledge can be judged or measured, but an attitude can only be observed in a few days or weeks. The moment I see incompatibility, I know I've made a mistake.

- In my previous company where I worked before starting my own, I remember a person who started working without a salary. He was undoubtedly talented and had the requisite skills and knowledge, but the one thing that stood out was this attitude and passion for believing in the company's vision, shown in the interview.

- *"Clock building, not time telling. Build an organization that can endure and adapts through multiple generations of leaders and multiple product cycles".*

- The author gives an example of Walt Disney, which evolved from creating cartoons to animation to television to theme parks.

- Closer home think about Reliance, Godrej, Piramal to L&T – all have progressed in all directions.

Title: Sell by Subroto Bagchi

The core idea behind this Book:

Subroto Bagchi presents the concepts of selling and salesmanship from his unique perspective.

Special Note:

A fantastic book highly recommended to anyone even remotely connected to sales.

Key Takeaways and What's in for us:

- *"Selling is a three-legged stool: part is an art, science and part is witchcraft, all in equal proportion."*

- When you dig deep in the book, he gives examples of how this is true. With algorithms, big data etc., working hard, it's a science for sure as marketers can now predict based on likes, views and browsing what and how to target their potential customers. It's an art because a good salesperson with excellent communication and personality can create a need on the spot of selling. Imagine you visiting a mall and only browsing through some pants or shoes. Reading your emotions with a pant or shoe already you are wearing, he will tell you features, style and comfort in a manner by which most of the time we end up buying. The salesperson with skills will figure out who the buyer is and what they must say. Selling is also witchcraft which caught my attention. A lot of selling is magic. He gives an example of a statement we often hear from someone who says, "he can sell an ice cream to an Eskimo." In sales terms, the phenomenal ability to sell is a combination of the vast knowledge of the art and the science of the selling process, intuition and personal character traits, through the power of persuasion, and a story is convincingly created to sell eventually.

- *"Every successful salesperson has his repertoire of interesting stories of unanticipated success, near misses and anti-climatic episodes in the prospecting process."*

- True. When I close my eyes and think from day one of my career till date, there is a story associated. Few have been cemented in my mind. The stories of my first sale, the rejections, the joy, the celebrations are all stories I cannot forget. The first purchase order, the extraordinary effort I put in a few, the journey to my international sales, etc., are all stories. As a reader, I urge you to start listing these of your career as you unknowingly already use them in a different context when you sell. Once you sharpen these, the prospecting process will only get simplified.

- *"When selling a product or service or an idea, you need to cut through the maze to locate the real prospects and shake hands with them."*

- Yes, knowing the goalposts precisely always helps. How often have we sometimes spent endless time and energy knocking on the wrong doors at the wrong people's places? We fall prey and get emotionally carried away as the other person has been good to us for years, but he is helpless, and obviously, he is not going to say that to you. You need to know the king, the tiger in the jungle, who will issue you that sale.

- *"Always dress up; do not dress down. You never know when your backside is up for public viewing. Always keep those shoes shiny and clean. You never know who you will meet today.* Your shoes will speak about the company you keep".

- You don't need great lessons to understand power dressing. Just read the above a couple of times and know what to do. We all understand the importance of good dressing, neat and clean hands, hygiene etc. but how many follow this seriously. You have those few seconds to make that impression, and you don't want to ruin those with inadequate preparation.

- *"The best salespeople see themselves as consultants who can advise their clients, bring teams together to create a solution and finally sell a solution with a consultative approach."*

- A brilliant sentence to inspire any salesperson. I've always looked at myself as the 'conductor' - someone who manages the orchestra. After understanding my prospect's needs, we try to get together people who can give them solutions, and in that process, the business also comes to us. Many times, we've not got business ourselves, but the right solutions given have won us the client forever as I've heard this many times from clients that "they are dying to work with us." Why would they make this sentence? They've seen the consultative approach, the unselfish attitude to put our customers interest ahead of everything. In the international markets particularly, the more I said, "No, your requirement doesn't fit in our product range," which has brought me more business later with them.

- *"Salespersons have to deal with the below stakeholders in every sale:*

- *The Vendor Selection Expert*: The first point of contact. Usually blocks new entrants but do not lose heart. Play innocent to win him slowly.

- *The Buyer*: The one who needs your product or service, quite an important person for you. He will have the most to say, but he may not be the end-user. He appears chained most of the time as he has to balance out many people internally.

- *The External expert*: Usually a consultant who comes into the picture. He will want to make his presence felt and will speak with knowledge and experience where he has delivered. His views will be valued the most.

- *The influencer*: You will be surprised; this person can be from an unknown territory you've not considered. Can be the CFO or even the HR head. Keep an eye on their body language as they speak less, but he will comment once you go from their office.

- *The Detractor*: He challenges the very strategy to buy the product or service. He has nothing against you but is not happy with the idea itself.

- *The Coach*: He is a part of the evaluation process and will be nice to you.

- *The Competition*: Always assume that there is something or someone you have overlooked. Know the past vendors, the wars and challenges they have gone through to anticipate moves.

- *The Lawyer*: He is the king of the master agreement. The lawyer's role is increasingly evolving to protect the deal, not just the client.
- You must also know who makes the payments? It is crucial to know the company's process from order placement to payments.

- *"People in sales must be supremely comfortable with the act of asking. Ask for direction, ask for leads, ask for referrals, ask for inside information, ask for a request for proposal, ask for the order and above all, ask for payments".*

- I've seen many salespersons not doing the above. They are shy to ask. They are good in their job, but the customer can take them for a ride if he identifies this trait that the salesperson doesn't have. These are the salespersons who do not know why and how they lost a deal. They always wonder when the tender was released and are ignorant of who pays their invoices. They are the ones who cut a sorry figure in internal sales meetings for payment collections and sales forecasting also.

- *"You should know how to lose well. "The team had been put on the proof-of-concept assignment has not quite measured up. The biggest reason given by the client was the team, though proficient, didn't ask the client enough critical questions. They simply delivered what was asked of them. The client felt if the delivery team just went by specifications and didn't question the assumptions behind the same, they wouldn't add any value to the final project."*

- This sentence shakes me up completely. A reason to lose a sale that hardly anyone has thought about. Adding value is important, and clients can reject you even if you have ticked on all other fronts.

- The author further says, don't stop here. A brilliantly worded letter or email to the client after you lose a sale is a fantastic suggestion he makes. Write a letter expressing what you learnt from the project you lost. Do not hesitate to say you are disappointed and appreciate the openness from the client to judge meritocracy. Mention in the letter that the briefing was good and ask for a potential opportunity that would come up shortly and mention that they can fall on you if required, even for the current project. This letter after losing is a brilliant strategy for long-term relationship building.

- *"Gratitude is a very powerful emotion. Expressing that goes beyond a thank you. Think of sending a handwritten letter, instead of asking a client for dinner, offer to host an offsite for a joint team from both the sides and request the customer to speak to them, a thank-you card can be sent, gift hamper or a book can be gifted."*

- A simple way to stay connected with clients even if there's no business happening currently. "I was thinking of you" is a statement I've used many times when I come across an industry update that may interest my client. I was thinking of you is a powerful statement you can use for sure.

Other Books I recommend reading:

Blue Ocean Strategy is a book published in 2004 written by W. Chan Kim and Renée Mauborgne, professors at INSEAD, and the name of the marketing theory detailed in the book. Blue ocean strategy is **the simultaneous pursuit of differentiation and low cost to open up a new market space and create new demand.** ... It is based on the view that market boundaries and industry structure are not a given and can be reconstructed by the actions and beliefs of industry players.

This book explains how companies work in red oceans where there's fierce competition and fight for market share and profits.

Blue Ocean Strategy is the holy grail of exploration typically where there is the first-mover advantage with no or little competition. This is often realized with an

"AHA" moment, a new invention or insight and few or limited businesses jump to explore and mine the vast potential. Sometimes, Blue Ocean markets/products are faced with a high entry barrier, thus keeping competition at bay. However, with the emergence of technology and globalization, most blue oceans turn red sooner or later.

Stories at Work by Indranil Chakraborty

Indranil Chakraborty has combined three qualities to pioneer business storytelling in India: two decades of experience leading teams and driving change at top firms like Unilever, Tata Group and Mahindra & Mahindra; a love for stories; and the entrepreneurial bug.

His firm, StoryWorks, has helped organizations and leaders harness the power of stories to create and deliver impactful messages. Since 2013, using the same approach outlined in *Stories at Work*, he has trained more than 1500 senior leaders in over thirty organizations, teaching them to be more effective in their communication.

Storytelling in business is different from telling stories to friends in a bar. It needs to be based on facts. *Stories at Work* will teach you how to wrap your stories in context and deliver them in a way that grabs your audience's attention.

The special tools, techniques and structures in this book will help you bring the power of stories into your day-to-day business communication. They will enable you to connect, engage and inspire, and ensure that everything you share has a lasting impression on your listeners.

The first book to document this change, ***Mavericks at Work,*** is business "edutainment" for an intelligent, ambitious readership, profiling some of the most exciting–and often eccentric–CEOs in the United States while detailing their remarkable strategies for success.

Who's going to write the next chapter in the saga of American business? Who's going to chronicle the best way to compete, the new way to win? That's the mission of Mavericks at Work, a book that profiles a network of rebels who are creating a new business model that makes use of new principles and captures what it means to be a state-of-the-art organization. This book is nothing short of a lively new intellectual plan for business including such pioneering companies as ING Direct, Southwest Airlines, Pixar, HBO, Anthropologie, Craigslist, Netflix, and Commerce Bank.

An activity you can do:

- List down top ten books you have read (or even more if you wish).
- Think about a little story you may have with each of the books. It could be a gift, a recommendation, a purchase you made out of interest but never completed, an author you love to follow or just a book you know had created a big hype during its launch.
- Write down the top five or more key takeaways from each of the books.

And the journey continues....

Who would have imagined how the world is today a good thirty years back when I started my career. I then read in the newspapers that India would be an economic power in this decade, and we can witness that. The world has added more technology, resources, capacities, opportunities, and so has it added several challenges.

As a marketer, a profession I love, I see a completely different way forward. The strategies would be different, the customers' psyche would evolve more, the usage of technology in marketing & sales would be altogether exciting, making the experience more informed and involved.

Just as I sit on my couch surrounded by my books, a cup of coffee, a notebook, and a pen in my hand, I hope to capture the next phase of my professional career in the coming time.

Thank you

9 789356 115095

Printed by Libri Plureos GmbH in Hamburg,
Germany